D1

This book is dedicated to all the women across the world who have experienced challenges in their lives and found the courage to succeed through those difficult moments. My hope for you is that you will continue to be brave, courageous, and unstoppable.

CONTENTS

DEDICATION   iii

CONTENTS   v

ACKNOWLEDGMENTS   vii

REKETTA C. WRIGHT   11
Undeniably Unstoppable

TAWANA ROWLAND   21
Unstoppable Faith

CHAKA KHAN COLLYMORE   27
Indestructibly Unstoppable

DENISE WIGGINS   37
Intentionally Unstoppable

DINA KNIGHT NELSON   47
Unquestionably Unstoppable

ERICA PERRY GREEN   55
Bodaciously Unstoppable

FELICIA A. GARRETT   65
Unmistakably Unstoppable

KAREN BONNER   75
Unconditionally Unstoppable

KIMBERLYNE ROUNDTREE   **85**
Fearlessly Unstoppable

LATASHA WILLIAMS   **95**
Purposely Unstoppable

MONICA LEWIS   **105**
Powerfully Unstoppable

NATROSHA MILLER   **115**
Undauntedly Unstoppable

RONKEYUNA GREEN   **123**
Triumphantly Unstoppable

SHEARESE STAPLETON   **131**
Victoriously Unstoppable

TRACEY WOLFE   **139**
Transformationally Unstoppable

CONNECT WITH US   **147**

ACKNOWLEDGMENTS

I would like to thank my Lord and Savior, Jesus Christ, without you I am nothing. I am thankful that you never left me. Thank you for blessing me with gifts to empower and transform lives. I am forever grateful for your pure love, grace, and favor.

To my parents: Pastor Levy Brown, Sr. and Prudie Brown. Your love and support means the world to me. Thank you for always praying for me. Your words of encouragement were always comforting. I am blessed by our relationship. Thanks for teaching me to remain humble and to be a great woman.

My dearest son Daniel Wright, IV. You are full of love and joy. You've taught me so much about myself. You are my greatest accomplishment. It's a joy to be your mother. I love you with everything in me. You are my daily inspiration.

To my brothers: Levy Brown, Jr. and Jonah Brown. I simply love you guys. Thanks for just being there. To my sweet sister-in-love, Elisa Brown. Thanks for your support and loving me.

My Pastor, Dr. Kevin A. Williams. Thank you for your spiritual guidance. Your leadership has been a blessing to my life. I'm appreciative of your constant support and encouragement.

To all of the co-authors who believed in me thank you. I am grateful for your commitment to this project. I pray many blessings over your lives as we are forever connected.

Special thanks to Tequita Brice and WriteIt2LIFE Publishing. You are truly a blessing to my life. Thank you for lending your expertise and helping me bring this collaborative project to life.

To Marcus and Tammy Battle of Battle Branding, thank you for your great work on this project.

To everyone that will purchase this book, thank you for your support. Thank you for reading our courageous stories.

REKETTA C. WRIGHT
Undeniably Unstoppable

I said "I do" in August 2009 to what I thought would be my forever, that is until the perfect picture started shattering piece by piece. All I ever wanted was a happily ever after. Shortly, I would learn that was not the divine plan. By 2014, my picture-perfect world began to show all the flaws and defects it had so craftily concealed for months before.

I had everything I thought I ever wanted. I was married, co-owned a thriving healthcare company, lived in a lavish home in the suburbs fully loaded with all the bells and whistles, drove a fancy car, secured the best school district for our children, and had a beautiful family. On the outside, we were the iconic family, but behind closed doors, our real lives were a completely different situation altogether. Despite what appeared to be me living the fairy tale life, I was powerless to stop the avalanche that started down the slope that was my life.

Having been an entrepreneur for over ten years, I was used to being able to control most things related to my business and future. However, at that time in my personal life, there were some pretty painful things happening that were completely out of my control. If I was being honest, there were many times in my marriage that I didn't deal with "the elephant in the room". Whether it was because I didn't want to start an argument, be told I was nagging, or because I simply didn't want to confront what I knew in my heart, the elephant stayed front and center until I was able to command it and make it trust me.

My elephants were several things happening simultaneously in my marriage at the same time. They ranged from being mistreated, lied to, cheated on, to being abandoned and deceived. When my husband and I would talk about an issue that had occurred to find a resolve, I would ask, "What made you do that" or "Why did you do that?" The answers he provided were always given in an attempt to make it seem as if I were somehow delusional and didn't know what I was talking about or they were lies altogether. It made me second guess myself, at times, and conclude that because he gave me an additional piece of information I didn't initially have, he must be telling the truth.

How many times have you ignored signs or allowed things to happen because you didn't want to confront the issue or face reality? That was me, A LOT! Typically, that was my go to option -- just ignore it and deal with it later. When later came, my thoughts told me I wasn't strong enough to address all the injurious things that were happening. I started listening to those negative voices and I became withdrawn, evasive, and removed. I distanced myself from my family, friends, and those who loved me the most. I didn't want to let anyone in my world of chaos that was spiraling out of control. I pretended everything was okay when it wasn't. My trips home were quick and time with friends was almost obsolete. When I did select to be around people or functions that my husband and I had to attend together, I became overwhelmed with thoughts about if we were going to get along while we were there, how could I hold his hand when I knew what he was doing, and the thoughts raced on and on. It was exhausting being around people pretending. It took so much energy making people believe everything was good. I told myself, "If I'm not around people, they won't know that my marriage and life is not so pretty". I was simply existing, stressed, exhausted, and depressed. I walked around my "perfect" home on egg shells because I was convinced anything I said would be the wrong thing and would spark an argument. So, I suppressed my feelings of hurt, anger, betrayal, and resentment just so I could try to keep my family together. I didn't want to be the one who broke us.

I put a lot of pressure on myself to be the wife who did mostly everything right. No, I wasn't perfect, but I honored my marriage and my family was my first priority. One night in January 2014, I was asleep and awoke to hear my husband getting ready to leave the house. Panicked, I sat up and asked, *"Where are you going?"* I just knew something wasn't right. He casually responded, *"Oh, out to the pool hall."* I thought to myself, *"why do have to go to the pool hall this time of night especially when you have a basement that was built with a pool table in tow for your entertainment"*. But it remained a thought that I dare not speak out of my mouth. So, I simply replied, *"Ok"* and tried to go back to sleep. Of course, sleep wouldn't come. Instead, I was angry with myself for not speaking up. I was left there with the kids like I was the live-in help but not the wife. Why was this happening to me? Exhausted from the tears, I eventually fell asleep.

At that point, our marriage was extremely fragile. We had issues of mistrust and poor communication. The next day, I was preparing dinner for our family while he was on a phone call with a business associate. His cell phone, however, was in the kitchen beside me. While I was prepping food, he received a text. The contact's name and message showed on the screen and I read it. Yes, I read the message which was what I should have been able to do in a healthy marriage. However, because ours was far from that, I was distrustful of him. I was like, "Who is she," again to myself.

I read the text in its entirety and immediately stopped what I was doing. Enraged, I raced into the room where he was on the phone and asked, *"Who is she and why did she send you this message about last night!"* I didn't care that he was on the phone. I had been disrespected in the most painful of ways. I asked him to get off the phone and told him we needed to talk NOW. He put his finger up and asked me to wait. I screamed, *"No get off the phone! They can wait!"* And we, immediately, went into conversation about the text message that was there right before my eyes.

It's one thing to hear a rumor or hear people talking, but it's quite another thing to see something for yourself. Right there in black and white, how could you deny or even ignore that? *"You lied to me! Remember last night when I woke up in a panic and asked where you were going? You said to the pool hall. But you didn't go to the pool hall, you went to see her!"* Caught, now, in his web of lies and deceit, he only responded, *"Reketta, I'm sorry."* Tears formed in my eyes. *"I'm your wife! How could you do that!"* He tried to hug me apologetically, but I broke away and ran into the bathroom so the kids wouldn't come in and see me. With my heart completely shattered, I leaned against the wall and fell to the floor sobbing. This was a hurt and a pain I couldn't possibly describe. I was numb.

I told myself I deserved better in a husband and marriage, but I didn't yet really believe that. I questioned myself and came up with a million reasons why I couldn't leave: I didn't have the money to get my own place, I would be a single mom, what would happen to the assets and the business we had together, how would this work for the children, and what in the world would other people say! I recycled those questions daily. Although I knew I was in an unhealthy relationship, I also knew I was dying mentally, emotionally, and spiritually. It seemed like I was in a hopeless place.

The year progressed and because I refused to make a decision about the marriage, things were only getting worse. We disagreed, constantly argued, lacked respect for each other, and had no connection. As a licensed therapist, I knew we couldn't continue in the direction we were going and recommended we seek professional counseling. Of course, that was a flat out no! He wasn't open to that suggestion but I was desperate for a change and I prayed and asked God what to do. I knew I couldn't continue to live a lie. It was not what I wanted my children to see and it was unhealthy for me. I needed Him to help me find answers.

Finally, in September, my husband told me he no longer wanted to be married. I felt like how dare he tell me he didn't want to be married. I should have been telling him that after all I'd been through. What did he mean he didn't want me? Hurt and devastated, I asked him to think about it and make sure that's what he wanted to do.

From September to December we simply existed like we were just roommates. As if it couldn't get any worse, he asked me to move out! At that point, I'd had enough. I began to earnestly pray and ask God to give me direction and guidance. Distressed, I went to look for an apartment for my son and I. It was like I had never had to negotiate anything before. Thank God, He was working on my behalf. I went in barely knowing what to communicate to inquire for an apartment when asked when I needed to move in. I told her as soon as possible. The only date that was available was December 30th. At that moment, something in me awakened. I gentled whispered and said, *"That's my birthday."* God has a way of showing us signs through people and things, we just have to be aware and in tune to receive them. Finally excited about something, I told her I would take it. I didn't tell anyone I was moving. I still wasn't ready for everyone to know fully what was going on in my marriage. Part of me hoped against hope that it was only temporary.

After I paid my deposits and got things in order, I

told my husband I was moving out on my birthday. You would have thought I was speaking Greek or something. He actually begged me to stay and went through all of these changes. Wait a minute, didn't you ask me to leave? But I wasn't falling for what I imagined was temporary guilt and remorse. I'd already overcome the fear of beginning the process of change in my life and I wasn't about to stop now. Truthfully, I was tired of being on the roller coaster. It was time to get off and try to gain some peace and normalcy apart through a separation.

On my birthday, I left my beautiful home with nothing but boxes of clothes, my puppy, and some personal items. I was starting all over again. I purchased everything brand new for my son and I. It was our new start. Somehow I had been in a fog of pity and self-doubt but suddenly I was awakened. I found strength, courage, and bravery to do what I once felt seemed like the impossible. If there was any chance of reconciliation, I truly hoped that my husband was willing to do the work to show me while we were apart.

One of my favorite scriptures is Proverbs 3:5-6, *"Trust in the Lord with all thine heart; and lean not unto thine own understanding. In all thy ways acknowledge him, and he shall direct thy paths."* My spirituality and relationship with God was always the foundation I leaned on when I didn't know what to do or how to do it. The strength that God gave me during that time was amazing. The new path He had me on, I didn't understand but I trusted Him. I walked away from what was comfortable but chaotic. That was not a recipe for a successful life, however, I got comfortable in the chaos.

For several months, no one knew I'd been forced to make the decision to move out. Someway, somehow, I'd hoped it would still work out. However, someone did find out. I was talked about, embarrassed, and ostracized. I felt so alone and I didn't understand why. I wasn't the one who had been unfaithful. I wasn't the one who told the other I didn't want to be married anymore and I wasn't the one who asked the other to move out. But I'd begun the process of healing and I was able to find peace in the midst of my storm.

Days passed and restoration started to begin. Through God's grace and professional counseling, I was able to forgive my husband, forgive myself, and move forward in my new life journey. I must say it was not easy, but it was another process of learning to trust myself, gain confidence, and find new strength and wisdom. I've learned so many lessons and so much about myself. I've become a better woman, mother, friend, sister, and entrepreneur. I gained my smile back, my joy was restored, and I found new purpose.

Despite the fact that my marriage fell apart, I still believe in love and I know one day it will find me again. I encourage anyone who is reading this to know that you are loved, God's grace is sufficient, and He will give you the strength you need to get through anything. Just trust Him when it looks difficult and know that He is right there with you. Before I didn't realize how powerful a woman I was, however, now, there is no question who I am. I am Undeniably Unstoppable!

About Reketta

Reketta C. Wright is a heart centered entrepreneur, licensed therapist, and motivational speaker who has touched the lives of thousands during her career. Reketta is known for her warm presence and personable touch.

Reketta is the owner of Wrights Care Services, a private counseling practice in Greensboro, North Carolina, that serves women and families in emotional healing, recovery, and transformation. She holds a Masters in Rehabilitation Counseling from North Carolina A&T State University and has been successful with creating a healthcare company from the ground up. She is the author and visionary of the book collaboration entitled Wake, Pray, Slay: A Woman's Guide to Being Unstoppable.

She is the proud mother of Daniel (5). She enjoys motherhood, philanthropy, and business. Reketta is living her life on purpose and is on a mission to empower and encourage others to live an intentional life.

To learn more about Reketta visit, www.rekettacwright.com.

TAWANA ROWLAND
Unstoppable Faith

How many times did I tell myself if I ever work this hard for anyone another day in my life it would be for me? At the time, I had no idea what I was speaking over my life nor did I have any idea the depth of my life assignment. With all the hours I was putting in and all of the money I was making, I became more convinced that there was so much more to me than just the ability to generate a bi-weekly paycheck. I knew God had something different planned for my life.

Initially, I was so happy when I got hired. I purposed to be one of the best workers they had ever seen. I had a six day 40 hour plus weekly schedule but I set in my mind to do more and to always go above and beyond what was asked of me. My salary increased from $10 to $23 an hour in just two years. Never experienced in my life, I had a job with no college experience making what I thought was more than a little change. You would think I had it made. On the outside, everything was all together but inside I was drained. I was making money but I didn't have a life. I was always tired and could never make my kids school or sports engagements.

Seniority played a huge part in my particular field. The more seniority gained, the less the workload. This was fair, right? Apparently not for me. After six years, I was still given the heavy workloads. Yearly performance evaluations were supposed to add an additional week of vacation and the opportunity to be rehired for another year. As hard as I worked, I didn't seem to be getting any of these benefits and I was getting frustrated. While all the other employees were waiting for the perfect timing to become permanent employees, I was constantly fighting just to be found good enough.

To cope with my unhappiness, I started partying. At least four days a week I was in the club. I would leave one club and go to another. I was known to turn the party out even if there was only one person in the room. What can I say? I loved to dance and I had an energy that made me loveable, fun and pleasant to be around. Then came October 4th, 2013.

I remember the day like it was yesterday. All day I had this feeling that something life changing was about to happen.

I didn't know it would be the day I would finally be free from the madness - the job that everyone saw as the perfect job, the job that everyone I encountered would always say I better not ever leave. I would say, "I know that's right. I ain't going nowhere!" but deep down I hated the job. I would rant to my coworkers about my life being worth more than what I was getting paid. "You can let them work you like that if you want but I am tired" I remember saying. I knew God had something better for me while I was making these statements but I had no idea losing this job was part of the plan.

After getting laid off I had plenty of time on my hands. Since I had already begun to party, I decided I had what it took to take it to another level and do something I liked. In a six-month time frame I put together over six events: white parties, open mic parties, and comedy shows. In addition to the larger parties, I would host weekly parties that were also really popular. The most highly attended ones were Eye-Candy Fridays (free for the ladies) and Hump-Day Wednesdays. Despite getting laid off from my job, I was having the most fun doing two things I loved: promoting parties and making money. This was so much better than that the job that I slaved at for six years.

I started hosting a community event called Fun Day Sunday at Warnersville Park. I would invite people out to the community park for fun and games. We brought popsicles and chips for the kids and bottled water for the guys playing basketball. For about a month, this was a regularly scheduled event. My family pitched in and helped me on Sundays at the park. The funny thing was that while I was hosting these Sunday events, I began to engage more and more with the children who attended. Spending time with them allowed me to see how smart and talented they were. I would look at them and see future doctors, lawyers, models, public speakers, and entrepreneurs. I was connecting with kids that had the potential to do so much that I felt compelled to do something it about it. But how? I didn't want them to fall victim to their surroundings or to end up another statistic.

After much self-examination, I realized the only way I could help these children was if I first changed myself. My life was not an example that I was particularly proud of at the time. Don't get me wrong, the parties showcased skills that I wasn't aware I had but I wanted to be more responsible. I wanted to be effective in teaching the children how to be leaders. I wanted to show them that they were more valuable than an hourly wage on a job they didn't really love. The passion I had was so real, I had no choice but to change. I wanted to make the biggest impact I could in these children's lives. I had to make a difference. So, I decided the best way for me to do this was to give my life to the lord, accept Christ as my savior and allow him to begin the change in me I needed to see. It was the best decision I ever made.

With my new-found freedom, I could finally see my way clear to follow the path of my life assignment I had been ignoring all this time. First, I hired a consultant to talk me through exactly what it was I wanted to do and how I wanted to do it. I went through a business startup program that assisted me with all the paper work for my 501(c)3. Twelve days from the date I applied, I got my approval letter from the IRS. Based on the work I'd already begun doing fulfilling my purpose, (hosting the community activities) they back dated my exemption status to 2013 and I was official! Now the party planner was planning youth empowerment events. Now the person who needed self-confidence was teaching confidence and leadership skills.

I realized sometimes in life we don't understand everything that happens to us especially when we think we have it all figured out. But I've learned that we will never have it all figured out. The vision over our lives is so much bigger than we can ever imagine. It was my passion that led me to my purpose. I had no idea I would start a non-profit organization. To tell you the truth, I had no idea what a non-profit organization was. God took the gifts he gave me and the things I was most passionate about and showed me how to walk in my purpose.

Six years of my life I worked a job just because I was

getting a nice check but I was so unhappy. Now I am the CEO of my own company and I do what I love. Whatever it is that you are passionate about, move towards it. Don't allow people to discourage you. Stay consistent with the process and you will find yourself...Unstoppable!

About Tawana

Tawana Rowland is a true testament to the something beautiful a life completely turned over to Christ can make. She is a youth leader with a passion to be an example to the next generation. She is a mentor and serves as a community activist in her community.

As the Founder of TSR Kids, an organization that provides mentorship and opportunities to underprivileged families and children in our community, Tawana is a mentor and desires to see these children succeed. The organization is designed to help children identify their talents and gifts and build confident, strong-minded young leaders. She was nominated Woman of the Year 2016 by Greensboro News and Record.

To learn more about Tawana visit, http://tawanastaynstrong.com.

CHAKA KHAN COLLYMORE
Indestructibly Unstoppable

I was four years old, it was Christmas, and all my siblings were sitting around singing. The youngest of seven siblings. I was sitting on my eldest brother's lap. It was my turn, and I remember using profanity. I didn't know any better, right? In unison, everyone yelled, and my brother told my parents. You would've thought I'd committed a felony. I hid myself from all the commotion. I even tried dodging the spanking that came afterwards.

As recounted in that incident, my childhood was filled with a mix of good times, laughter, pain, shame and confusion. As a family, we attended church weekly, sung in the choir, enjoyed meals, and prayer together. My father was a recreational sports coach and my brothers were on most of his teams. One day my sister and I were at home with someone who should not have been there. He began to touch us inappropriately and asked us to perform oral sex on him. We had absolutely no idea what he was asking. As our minds whirled with confusion, he demonstrated what he wanted. Although he never mentioned to us not to tell anyone, we knew that this was convoluted. Feelings of shame and guilt gripped my entire body and heart. He never asked again. I assumed that he must've felt the same guilt and shame as I.

I continued to try to live as normal as possible but I couldn't seem to escape the abuse. I was molested by teenagers who were much older than I. They would lure me into their homes and bedrooms while they were home alone, or I'd be invited into the woods for a quick fondling violation. As skinny as I was, I had nothing that was appealing or that a man would be interested in or so, I thought. I was not looking for the kind of attention I received, but it always found me.

Being physically abused became a weekly routine, so much so that I began to think it was the normal. I constantly battled whether to keep my secret shame concealed or risk openly expressing it to someone who may or may not believe a word I was saying. Of course, I kept it all in hiding every feeling and concealing the pain.

For about two years my mother left our home to live in the city limits. I was an emotional mess. I had no clue of what was going on. I felt rejected and abandoned. My father took us every Sunday so that she could braid our hair. When it was time to leave, I cried like a newborn being snatched from its mother's womb knowing I couldn't stay. I just couldn't understand why she'd leave us that way. Later, she explained that she was depressed and needed time to rediscover who she was. She was raped when she was fifteen and the choice to keep the baby coupled with the demands of a husband and more children were too much for her to bear.

After my mom left us, rebellious decision-making and survival skills became my norm. This was definitely a defining moment in my life. I was a skinny twelve-year-old with noticeably crooked teeth who was afraid to speak or smile from a bike accident that chipped and shifted them. That didn't stop me from being seen. It was a given because of where my friends and I chose to hang out. I became, what I thought was, a functioning dysfunctional. I thought I had learned the essence of masking pain, insecurity and shame. I became critically comical. If a guy approached me, I just cut him down with the look on my face or with my words. This was an unfortunate trait I learned from my mother She was the queen of impudent words. She could say things that would leave you thinking you'd just been sliced with a switch blade.

My father passed away at the age of 46 when I was nineteen. He had heart disease which caused him to have a major heart attack. He was young, had only one wife, seven children, and worked diligently daily without complaining. My father was my hero and represented the epitome of an authentic man. I watched my father take on every responsibility with a smile. Yes, he fussed, but he always found a good reason to do it. He had so much compassion for the well-being of others. Once one of our neighbor's sons was put out in the cold and living in the car. My father opened our home to him even though we were already nine people deep in a three-bedroom small ranch style home. I constantly witnessed his kindness and selflessness to others during the years of his life. I was and am a daddy's girl. He was the steer, solidarity, protection, and everything that I and my family needed. The attributes my father exemplified would later be the deciding factor in my choosing a lifetime mate.

After my father's passing, I was not in a good place. I found myself contemplating suicide. My heart was broken. I felt like everything that my father stood for died right along with him. There was no reason for me to live without him. Again, I used pain as my scapegoat. I had given myself a license to run away from my deeply rooted issues and hide from what could undoubtedly liberate me.

Every relationship I found myself in showcased my insecurities and my need to keep a guy in my life. Whether it was ongoing or an every-now-and-then relationship, I always felt dissatisfied. I wanted more and I knew that there was more for me, I just didn't know how to go about getting it. It wasn't until I was in a pivotal relationship that exposed the real issue in my decision making that I finally gave myself the permission to look within. My mother would be the one to applaud for this. One day my boyfriend and I walked into my home. Seated there when we walked in, my mother said to me, "Muffin (my nickname)! You're hurting yourself." Unable to yet connect my actions to what others were seeing, my response was, "Mom! No, I'm not!" It would take me a couple of years to realize what mom could see then that I could not.

As an adult, I was self-medicating with men. Still grieving

the death of my father, I became pregnant with my first child and I couldn't have been happier. I had a great pregnancy. No morning sickness. Eating was simple, I only gained twelve pounds, and I was as happy as I could be. At twenty-six weeks, I left my usual check-up. The baby was kicking and growing as expected. What could possibly go wrong?

A week later, late on a Friday night, I started feeling extremely weak. My sister came to get me and rushed me to the emergency room. When we arrived, my body temperature was 108 degrees and the baby had no heartbeat. Unbeknownst to everyone, my doctor discovered that I was in labor and the baby was deceased in my womb. Numb, my sister began to cry and I consoled her. At the time, my emotions were frozen. I was in shock.

The next day I awakened with the rush of all those emotions I should have had the night before, now overwhelming me. I was crying uncontrollably, I had a terrible headache, and I was plagued with thoughts of suicide. You see, when I found out that I was pregnant, I quickly committed to move from my third floor apartment and purchase a two-story townhome. The reality of having to return to that empty home alone without the sole purpose of why I made the purchase was almost too much to bear.

There were many reasons I could have been celebrating. I was the first of my siblings to ever purchase a home and with just my high school education, I worked diligently to become debt free before doing so without the help of my parents. But I wasn't feeling very celebratory. All I wanted to do was sulk. I also felt like the one that was left out. Out of seven siblings, I was the one who had no children. I was furious, hurt, disappointed, and pained all over again. It took me having an identity crisis to yield the change I needed to experience in my life - a very intentional and intimate relationship with God.

After losing my child, I decided to desist from making rebellious decisions. I decided to make some changes and I started with me. From finishing school late, never completing college, to being in numerous unhealthy and ungodly relationships, all were my outward expressions of the inner healing I needed. I faced what had made me 'the girl who loved hiding'. Although it was very challenging, this meant no more excuses, blaming, or aborting what had the potential to be successful, and embracing my opportunity to finally and liberally enjoy life. The determination came after a much needed wake up call.

I began to find freedom through the Word of God. I had

one friend and accountability prayer partner that helped me through that part of my journey. I was alone but not lonely. I began to understand that born again believers were not exempt from the fluctuations of life but I didn't have to be bound by them. I yielded it all to God so that I could live in the victory God's Word promised. It was at that point, my entire life began to thrive. I was experiencing my turning point. I was completely healed from all my hurts, pains, and insecurities instantly.

It's been five years since I married a man who knows and loves God with all his heart. He knows all about my past and chose to love me and to be my king forever! He has proven to be the covering suited for my life. We have the privilege of partnering together and living triumphantly! The life for me that was like the Underground Railroad, I confronted and overcame. I dismantled the lies I once lived by. I willingly sought God for liberty, healing, and restoration and He awakened me to the indestructible and unstoppable life that was planned from the very beginning.

About Chaka

Chaka Khan Collymore is the owner and operator of Excellent Cleaning Services, LLC, and Co-Founder of Harvesters, in Zebulon NC. As part of her servitude to The Lord, Chaka serves in ministry, volunteers in her community the aid of the elderly and widows. Chaka knows that God's unconditional love is available to all mankind. She has purposed in her heart to continue to display His love with her captivating smile that greets everyone joyfully, through acts of kindness, all while sharing the Gospel of Jesus Christ.

To learn more about Chaka visit, www.harvestersnc.com.

DENISE WIGGINS
Intentionally Unstoppable

The day I let my mother down was one of the worse days of my life. No doubt about it, I crushed her heart. Me, the one who was named after her mother, Fannie, because she was so smart and industrious. I was supposed to be that way too. "Live up to that name", my mother would always say. Not that the name Fannie is equivalent to some earth-shattering event. No, Grandma Fannie stood for everything that was right about our family. This woman alone raised dozens of children (her own as well as those of other relatives and neighbors) with the strength and tenacity of two people.

My mother always made a point of talking about how strong Grandma was. I remember once when I phoned home and cried about my seemingly never-ending struggles and questioned why I was going through, she comforted me with stories of Grandma's strength. "You're made like your Grandma Fannie", she said. "She faced a lot of hard times, too, but they made her who she was and they will do the same for you. You'll get through them because she did. You're the strongest of all my kids because you have the strength of your Grandma Fannie. That's why you have her name." Most times that small reminder of how much I was like Grandma rejuvenated me and I would be ready to move on again. Not this time.

When Dr. Catherine confirmed my mother's suspicions that her perfect teenage baby girl was pregnant, the news broke her heart. It also presented a new worry for me. The magnitude of her hurt and disappointment created an atmosphere of tension and distance between us—neither of which I was used to. I wanted *so* much to talk to her to tell her how I was feeling. I wanted her to know how sorry I was that I hurt her and how I needed her to tell me everything was going to be all right. But after the visit to the doctor, she barely said a word to me.

My mother had her first child at fifteen years old then four more concurrently each year after that. So you can see why she was so strongly against us getting pregnant before we got married. Eventually her distance proved too much for me, and I suffered a stroke.

I remember the right side of my face being paralyzed, my eyes blinking uncontrollably, and being unable to shut them when I wanted to. My face was totally distorted, making eating, drinking, and talking more like chores. I could not believe what was happening to me. First, I felt like my youth had been ripped away from me and now this.

I wasn't a very religious person then, but I was smart enough to believe there was a God. I wondered where He was for me. I was scared to death of what was happening to my body and desperately needed Him to stop the hurt and drive away the fear. Most of all, I needed God to make my mother talk to me again because I missed her so much.

A few months into the paralysis and pregnancy, my doctor warned my mother that the stroke might affect the health of my baby. Shortly after this news, my mother and I began to talk again. I think the news startled her. I know it did me. But I didn't care. She was talking to me again. The paralysis was healing and I was enjoying this small window of peace.

After my son was born, my relationship with my mother changed again. She did not like the idea of my child's father still being in my life and this would set off a barrage of arguments between the two of us. The mental and emotional abuse I was going through with the father of my two youngest children worsened and everything in my life spiraled out of control. There I was with a child out of wedlock at 19 plus two more before I was 30 years old. I had no career. I was working dead end jobs unable to make ends meet. I had hurt my mother to the core of almost no return and now here I was having to move back home. If I had only listened. As I learned the hard way, parents can see things we can't see. If I had known the hell that awaited me in advance I would have listened, but then I think back to part of the process.

I always had a desire to be an entrepreneur. I knew I needed to make some changes in my life to be completely successful, I just didn't know how. Once home, my mother spoke positive things into my life and everything in me began to change for the better. I started to see myself in a different light and I began to dream again. With some coaxing, my mother convinced me to move to North Carolina. The cost of living there was much cheaper than being in D.C and she knew I always wanted to purchase a home for myself and the children. I left my oldest son with his father in D.C., packed up the two youngest, and made my move.

Because I hadn't broken any of my destructive life patterns, I continued to choose abusive men and ended up in dysfunctional relationships. I had to break out of this destructive cycle before I lost my mind. When I hit rock bottom I wanted something different and I knew a relationship with God was my answer.

I found a great church where the kids and I would go every Tuesday for bible study and Sunday service. There, I began to deal with all the hurt and bitterness I was holding on to. The more I read my word and grew closer in relationship with Christ the more I was able to forgive. I forgave all the men in my life for all the hurt and pain they caused. I moved pass all the bitterness all these relationships had left in my life and focused on my healing. My relationship with Christ and my children became my sole priorities.

I made some major changes in my life, from how I thought to the people I hung around. I started wanting more and reawakened the dreams that had long lay dormant in my spirit. I wrote my vision boards and pushed towards becoming an entrepreneur. I surrendered to the complete restoration that was taking place in my life and opened myself up to everything I desired. I aligned myself with the right people, opened my first mental health facility, and strategically positioned myself to meet the love of my life.

It happened when I was traveling home with a friend whose car broke down unexpectedly leaving us stranded on the side of the road at the mercy of fast-moving drivers. For a while, no one stopped to help us. That is until Mr. Daryl Wiggins showed up.

He had a very kind face and after telling him what the problem was, he set about fixing it. I was immediately drawn in to his kind face and voice to match. As I was admiring our rescuer, a little voice inside me cautioned me to draw back. *Don't even think about it. You'll just get hurt again.* As I tried to dismiss him out of my mind, my girlfriend stated that she noticed him watching me. "He sure likes you," she said in a sing-songy voice as she started her car. To that I replied, "Girl, please. I'm not even going there. I'm fine just like I am." Of course, she didn't buy that. She knew me well.

She noticed he hadn't driven off yet so she got out of the car and ran back to his. I slid closer to the rear-view mirror and tried to pull it toward me without breaking it. I just had to see what was going on. Tammy stooped down a little as she talked. At one point, she pointed toward her car. *Why is she pointing this way*, I wondered? Before I could answer myself, I saw our kind helper hand her a white piece of paper. Tammy took it and wrote something on it and handed it back to him. Then he handed her another piece of white paper. I could hear her giggling as she gladly took it. A few seconds later, she stood up straight, gave him a quick wave and made her way back to the car. She had given him my number and he told her that he would give me a call.

True to his word, Daryl called that night. Trying not to appear anxious, I picked up on the fourth ring. He introduced himself again and I did the same. After a few awkward pauses with both of us trying to talk at the same time, the butterflies settled, and we had a lively conversation. He told me about his family. I told him about mine. He told me what he did for a living and I did the same. A few phone calls between us later and we were sharing deeper thoughts and desires for our individual lives. Daryl proved so easy to talk to.

You're probably thinking by now I fell hard for Daryl. You're absolutely right, beloved. I did. A few weeks after that first phone call, Daryl and I began dating. I felt like a girl all over again with him. I was giddy and school-girl silly. Whenever we were apart, I would miss him like crazy and become impatient for another visit. He was so different from all the other men I had ever met. First, he was then and is now a serious servant and lover of the Most High God. None of the other men in my life thought much about God. On our dates, he would talk about God—but not to the point of being fanatical. No, Daryl had balance to his conversations about God and other things. I enjoyed listening to him connect scriptural references to what was happening in his own life. Because I had learned from my pastor to do the same, I could relate to what Daryl was saying and could chime in with my interpretations. Then together, we talked about the Word of God. Being able to relate to him spiritually made knowing Daryl even more endearing. You would have had to be blind not to realize that he loved God more than anything anyone else or anything else in the world. I wouldn't have wanted it any other way.

Secondly, Daryl placed God ahead of everything else. I found I didn't mind coming in second to our Heavenly Father because it was God who made Daryl the man he is. For that reason, Daryl did all the things my former lovers never thought about doing. He always opened the car door for me, he loved me unconditionally, and he genuinely cared about my children. In time, I began loving this special man with all my heart.

God gave me a second chance at getting things right and Daryl and I got married a few years later. By the time he came into my life, my relationship with God had grown from liking Him a lot to having an intimate, genuine love for Him. This intimate love satisfied me fully. The trust that I placed in myself, I transferred it to God. I stopped the pity partying and I gave Him my anger, bitterness, and frustrations. I even gave Him all my pitiful religious efforts to do well. In turn, He gave me His peace.

My life as I look back has not been an easy journey, but I wouldn't change anything about it. As I sit to share my tough times to my good times, it brings me so much joy and peace because now I understand it was all necessary. It was part of the process to bring me to this place today. I say all that to say, do not rush through your struggles. Do not complain while you are going through. Count it all joy, because the victory on the other side will lead you straight to being truly...Unstoppable!

About Denise

Denise Wiggins has been in the healthcare field for over 8 years. She owns two Mental Health facilities in Atlanta, GA and Portsmouth, VA. and her own cosmetic line, Lipsynk Cosmetics, which launched in 2014. Denise founded a non-profit organization, Solo Mom Makeover Foundation, as empowerment for single mothers. She is the author of the book *My Struggle's, God's Glory* and won Philanthropist of the year award in 2016. Recently, Denise launched the Power Tour to inspire women to move into their purpose. Denise is set to film and be one of the executive producers of her first documentary in late 2017.

Denise was raised in Washington, D.C. and currently resides in Knightdale, N.C. with her husband, Mr. Daryl Wiggins, a blended family of five children, which includes two college students, and three grandchildren.

To learn more about Denise visit, www.denisewiggins.com.

DINA KNIGHT NELSON
Unquestionably Unstoppable

Growing up in the projects, all the families knew and respected one another. We addressed older relatives with Aunt or Uncle followed by their first name and we addressed older women or men Mrs. or Mr. followed by last name. Our house was always clean. We had plenty of food and had great birthdays and Christmas'. We were well mannered and our clothes were neat and clean. Although we were on public assistance, we didn't know poverty.

My mother was a single parent which was pretty much the norm for the projects during that time. Most homes had absentee fathers. For my life, it was also a perpetual family cycle as my mom grew up without her father in the home. This didn't stop her from being the best mother she possible could. She was very protective, giving, and demonstrated her love for us in a special way. She was also very strict and structured.

As with most families with children, in our house we had chores. I was the oldest of three, therefore, I was solely responsible for ensuring the chores were completed to the standards my mother required. If not, I was the one who got the whipping. My mom worked third shift, so there were many days we couldn't go outside and play with our friends. We had to watch them play from the window in our room. We were upset, disappointed, and cried many days. If that wasn't enough, we were picked on and frowned upon by other kids who had that privilege.

My father chose other avenues and lifestyles. At a young age, he was in and out of juvenile detention centers. Once he aged out of juvenile detention, he was in and out of correctional institutions. Growing up I hated him. I know how harsh that sounded but I remember crying nonstop whenever I was in his presence. When he would call, I would say just enough to get him off the phone. I didn't understand how he could say that he loved me, but wasn't there for me. I constantly beat myself up with a barrage of unanswerable questions: Why did he choose to do those things? Why wasn't he here for my protection? Why wasn't he here to take me to the candy store or take me on trips? Why wasn't he here for me to sit on his lap while he read me a book or helped me with my homework? I wanted so desperately for him to be a part of my life, to protect me from life like a father should.

I was bullied so badly I developed low self-esteem. No self-confidence caused me to walk with my head held down, body slouched with my neck facing forward. I was constantly getting in fights and picked on because I had dark skin, I was tall, I wore glasses, and I had big teeth. I got my glasses pulled off, was teased mercilessly, and called black bone and ugly simply because children can be so cruel. Because my dad, my protector was nowhere to be found, my hatred for him grew even stronger.

I carried the lack of self-confidence, low self-esteem and hatred for my dad for many years. I tried to commit suicide multiple times. I masked the fears I harbored and the internal struggles I battled through adolescence and well into adulthood. Most of the time, I felt like an outcast but that didn't stop me from being surprised if anyone showed interest in me. If a guy told me I was pretty or cute and wanted my number, I was in love. I lived in a fairy tale wishing and hoping, waiting and dreaming. Every relationship I had, I feel deeply in love, often getting used, abused and taken for granted in the process. Break-ups were not only depressing, they were heart breaking. They left me with a shattered heart every time. I was bleeding internally. It left me numb.

As a child, I had no escape from the pain but age provided me a momentary exit. When I got older, I mixed alcohol and pain medications to get me drunk and high. Being an emotional zombie was the only way I felt I could deal with the war going on in my mind. I blamed my dad because he was the first man to hurt me. After all, he abandoned me. He was the reason I attracted men that were damaged and never had a healthy relationship. There was an emptiness in my soul that I just wanted filled and trying to fill it lead me down a road I wasn't prepared for. Although I was considered an adult by all definitions of the law, at twenty-one years old, with no husband, father, or covering, I found myself pregnant.

However, nine months after I brought my daughter into the world, I met the gentleman who later became my husband. He was totally different than any man I had ever been with. He didn't smoke, drink or club. He was selfless, encouraging, committed, genuine, and honest. He listened, inspired, lead, and gave me much respect. He embraced me and my daughter as his own and filled me with a love I didn't think I would ever experience or even deserved.

My life changed dramatically after I got married. I gave my life to Christ and we added two beautiful girls to our family. In my new family unit, I witnessed the love, support, nurture, protection, passion, and guidance my husband had towards our daughters. It ignited something in me. It made me want to look past the rejections, hurt, and disappointments I felt towards my dad. I began to desire for him to be a part of my life as well as my family's life. I wanted him to meet his son and his grandchildren. It happened sooner than I thought.

One day after getting home from work, I was met by a man standing in my yard smoking a cigarette. I asked, "How may I help you." He responded, "I'm waiting for my friend to come out." I don't know but something in me knew that his friend was my dad. I screamed, ran into the house and jumped into his arms. He was just as surprised and excited as I. He asked me to forgive him and suggested we start a new relationship. The feeling was mutual and I was more than happy to oblige.

Things went well in the beginning, then I gradually began to see a change. His actions spoke louder than his words. Most days, I didn't know what he would say. Because he was fresh out of prison, he didn't have much. As his oldest daughter, I didn't want him to want for anything so I gave to him freely. But it didn't take long for him to subject me to his manipulation, broken promises, and lies. He used and took me for granted. He preyed on the fact that I was patient, forgiving and wanted him to be a part of my life. Then, I realized it was a cycle. It was the same cycle just with a different face. He was no different from the men I loved from my past. In my search for answers, I wondered why was this happening to me again? What in me was attracting these spirits?

Have you ever loved or felt you needed someone so bad you lost yourself in the process? You gave all of yourself and you got nothing but heartache, heartbreak, and disappointment in return? You thought they had your heart but you saw they were nothing like you. In fact, you saw that they were heartless and insensitive.

I cried to the Lord to fix it, heal it, expose it, pleading that he do something quickly. "*Restore my soul Lord! Restore my soul Lord, please restore my soul*", I prayed constantly. Just when I thought I was free from the residue of all the pain I felt as a child, it resurfaced. Allowing my dad back into my life re-introduced all the pain, agony, and angst. In fact, I think this pain was greater.

"*Many are the afflictions of the righteous one, but the Lord Jehovah delivers him from all of them. And he will keep all his bones that not one of them will be broken*" Psalms 34:19-20. I was in a bad place but I knew I didn't want to be there. More importantly, I knew I couldn't stay there. So, I did everything I could think of. I cried, I prayed, I fasted, I worshipped and I praised. I just wanted to be free; free from the pain, free from the torment, and free from the strain.

I gave myself over to the process of forgiveness. I spoke forgiveness out of my mouth daily. I forgave them and I forgave myself. My prayers became more specific. As the Holy Spirit exposed the raw areas of my life, I gave them to God to be completely healed, delivered, and set free. It didn't take long. Gradually, I experienced a calmness of peace in my spirit and restoration came physically, emotionally, and spiritually.

God restored me back to His original creation of me inside and out. Everything that was tarnished, damaged and broken was restored. I was able to see the unique, authentic and valuable beauty in Dina. Suddenly, all my struggles had meaning and purpose. There was a plan and an actual reason why I had to struggle through my pain. Through it, I realized my past didn't define me, it only directed me straight into my destiny. I understood that everything I endured wasn't just for me, it was to be used to help someone else.

When God has spoken over your life, the enemy will try to kill your promise. Every assignment has a birthing place and when there is a mandate on your life, pain and struggle is part of the process. The idea is to keep pushing forward. You can't give up even when it seems unbearable. My Father in heaven is the only true healer, mind regulator, and heart fixer. The old folks used to say He is the mender of a broken heart.

I can truly say He did what I asked. He lifted me out of my pit of despair and restored me Dina. His Dina: the Dina that was chosen for destiny, the Dina that he made over, completely new, the Dina that was Unquestionably Unstoppable!

About Dina

Dina Knight Nelson is a motivational speaker, minister, model, and author. She is the founder of Chosen for Destiny®, an organization that inspires women of all ages to live on purpose, offering opportunities for weekly girl talks with adolescents in local communities to share lectures of beauty, confidence, self-worth, bullying, relationships, etiquette to help them embrace a love for themselves. Her own personal story is true proof that success is not about resources. It is about being creative, open to change, faithful, resourceful, accountable and responsible. Her format of facing your fears head on, embracing your past, dealing with hurt and let downs head on, and envisioning your future has become a standard in her teachings and speeches. She tells those with open eyes, open hearts, and open minds, "Everything we go through is for someone else and we overcome by the words from our testimonies."

To learn more about Dina visit, www.dinaknelson.com.

ERICA PERRY GREEN
Bodaciously Unstoppable

A s I look back over my life, I can truly say that my life has been BLESSED! I was blessed to enjoy a wonderful childhood and be raised in a loving home with two wonderful parents. I was blessed to attend a prestigious university where I graduated at the top of my class. I was blessed to quickly secure a coveted job as a pharmaceutical representative. Soon after starting my career at age 25, I was blessed to marry my high school sweetheart, an analytical chemist, and discover that we were expecting our first child. Everything was falling into place and life was good.

Many times, the world has trained us to envy those that

look like they have it all together. We look on social media and see all these gorgeous pictures of successful people with beautiful families. These people look like they have it all together and don't have a care in the world. They make life look oh so easy. You see, the world would have you to believe that these people are perfect. In fact, many often commented that I was one of these very people.

From the world's view, I was always smiling with my amazing husband and daughter, traveling the world or accepting awards for various professional successes. But peeling back the layers of my life would quickly show you that my life has been filled with great trials, much-needed transformation, and overwhelming triumph.

Zoya Nicole Green was the name that we picked for our little princess. As we looked at our ultrasound pictures, we were overjoyed. I couldn't wait to hold my precious little girl and pour all of my love onto her. Everything was blissful, that was, until the day our dream turned into a nightmare.

After close to seven months of pregnancy, I found myself in a hospital fighting for my life and the life of our daughter. My blood pressure shot up to over 200/110 and my body was seizing convulsively. The prognosis was grim. My own doctor, thinking I would stroke out and die, turned my case over to the hospital attending and walked away. They literally thought that death was imminent.

I will never forget the account of that day. The day that shifted the rest of my life and left an invisible scar on my heart that no surgeon could repair. The day I experienced the greatest heartbreak of my life. The day I kissed my daughter for the first and last time.

It was August 4th when my healthy pregnancy quickly turned into a horrible tragedy. In the blink of an eye, I went from planning our nursery to holding my lifeless daughter in my arms. I used all my strength to sit up and kiss Zoya goodbye. As I looked down at her tiny face, I remember thinking how much she looked like her dad.

The months that followed were full of darkness as I fought through depression, guilt, hurt and anger. While these months were the most difficult of my life, they drew me closer to God in a most miraculous way! I could feel His presence with me through the darkness and depression. I felt Him championing me, *"Keep fighting. There is more for you to do."* It was my relationship with Him that gave me the desire to keep living, keep moving, and keep pushing. In the difficult times, I realized a strength I didn't know I had. In the six months after losing Zoya, I found the true meaning of turning it over to God.

As God brought me through my loss, He began to restore things in my life. We moved to Raleigh, N.C., purchased our first home, and I received a promotion on my job. While I didn't forget my daughter - my angel, I realized the supernatural power that helped me through my most challenging times. I also saw that all I had to do was activate my faith and watch God begin the process of restoration in my life. God started using me even through my pain. He used my testimony to warn other expectant moms of the signs and symptoms of Eclampsia. He used me to help save their babies.

After our experience, my husband and I were shocked at the many couples drawn to us for inspiration. These were families facing their own loss. We received numerous thank you messages from grieving mothers thanking us for sharing our story. We shared how we chose to honor Zoya yearly to help other families going through the same dark journey. Although it all seemed unfair at the time, God used my journey to bless many. Most of whom I didn't even know until years later. While we might not always understand the why, know that God always has a plan.

Before I knew it, I was sitting in my doctor's office in shock to find out that I was expecting again! I was in shock because the doctors told me that I probably wouldn't be able to have another child after Zoya. While the doctors gave up on me becoming a mom, God had other plans. Eight months later Camryn Nicole Green was born.

The next five years of my life were filled with pure

happiness and joy. My family flourished and we were blessed. But we all know that life is full of seasons and this season was coming to an end.

As Camryn's fifth birthday drew near, my health began to fail. After half a dozen appointments and numerous tests, the doctors finally admitted the virus they previously diagnosed me with was a mistake. Not only had they missed a severe strep infection but it lingered long enough to seep into my blood stream causing a deadly blood infection and irreversible damage to my heart. They gave me just three months to live without treatment. Now my life had been threatened before, but with this trial the devil surely plotted to take me out! After months of treatment, my cardiologist determined that I would need open heart surgery. I was well aware of the risks and the possibility of leaving my daughter without a mother and my husband without his wife.

As I suffered through the medications, the vomiting and the severe shortness of breath, I gained a deeper understanding of my own mortality and the real meaning of "life is short". I became fully aware of just how precious life was and of all the little often unnoticed gifts along the way. In those days, before my surgery, I took nothing for granted. Every breathe, every word, every moment with my family was more precious than gold. I focused on what really mattered and purged the rest.

As they wheeled me into my eight-hour open-heart surgery, I felt no fear, only peace. While I knew the danger and rate of survival, God touched my inner heart and gifted me with a calm like I had never experienced before. I literally felt him holding my heart. I knew that everything would be okay. He reminded me again, *"you still have work to do."*

During my surgery, my heart was stopped my heart for 8 hours. For eight long hours, I lay on a table kept alive by an artificial machine. My blood pumped to my vital organs as they worked to mend my damaged heart. While the surgeons worked vigorously to save my life, God was perfecting everything concerning me. My heart required a deeper repair than was possible on the operating floor. A renovation was taking place that only the Master Creator could facilitate.

Two days later, I awoke from surgery to see my doctors standing over my bed, cheering in amazement. My experimental surgery was God's latest miracle. I was still alive! God orchestrated my situation so that no one could get the glory for this work but Him! Once again, He positioned miracles in the midst of my storm. I remember my husband saying, "Babe, they all gave up on you, but you are still here for a reason." Those words and the quiet whispers of God kept me sane. During my darkest moments in life, God kept me alive. He kept me here.

Many wonder why I proclaim my heart surgery as the

best thing that ever happened to me. God gifted me with a renewed determination and clarity of purpose. He also gave me a boldness like I never had before. I now stood, unfazed by the world, ready to proclaim my testimony to anyone that would listen. I boldly gave Him all the glory.

Before the age of thirty-two, I had almost died twice, held my life-less first-born daughter, faced the darkness of depression, lost a six-figure income job and suffered through an eight-hour open-heart surgery. I had a long scar stretching across my chest and many unseen scars that only God and time could heal. Through the tears and setbacks, I learned how to stop looking at my scars as shameful badges of my past and see them as proud war wounds. Today, I do not hide my wounds, covering them up in shame, but rather wear them proudly, as an outwardly symbol of all that I have overcome.

Yes, my story conveyed to you an extraordinary testament of God's wondrous love. I now know that my life's journey was not just for me. While it gave me insurmountable strength and determination, it also gave me an unshakable faith. My journey, my trials, and my triumphs birthed a powerful testimony to bless others. My job was to tell what God had done for me and let others know that if He did it for me, he could do it for them.

I learned to count my blessings during my storms.

Throughout my life-threatening ordeals, I learned that there are blessings at every step of the journey. Even in your darkest hours, God can gift you with miraculous life-long revelations and shower you with indescribable peace. The great thing about His blessings is that they are eternal. The world didn't give them to you and the world can't take them away!

My smile often hid extraordinary pain, loss, fears and heartaches. The joy that I have now is not an earthly gift but rather given to me by my Heavenly Father. It was birthed from overcoming my trials. It left me with an understanding of what a life full of the blessings looks like.

Everything I went through brought me to my richest relationship with God. Even in my darkest hours, I felt God holding me and loving me back to life. All I had to do was ask Him to help me through the darkness. *"Whatever you ask in my name, this I will do, that the Father may be glorified in the Son. If you ask me anything in my name, I will do it"* John 14:13-14.

Many often asked me, "You've been through so much to be so young, how do you keep smiling?" My answer is always simple, "God kept me!" There is nothing more devastating than losing a child, but there is also nothing that reveals your inner strength and God's true love, like pushing through great pain.

Moving on is never easy. If you are dealing with grief or

loss, the best way to move on is to take it one moment at a time and remember, you are never alone. No one wakes up one morning completely healed or completely over what they have been through. Grief is a process and you have to allow yourself to grieve, but find comfort in knowing that there is truly nothing that God can't bring you through. If He brought you to it, He can bring you through it to be truly Unstoppable!

About Erica

Erica Perry Green is truly a woman who has risen from trials to triumph! An accomplished healthcare professional and business leader, Erica has an innate passion for helping others. She is a graduate of The University of North Carolina's School of Public Health where she has worked for over a decade in the corporate sector in Pharmaceutical Sales, Physician Training, Healthcare Sales & Marketing, and currently as a Regional Healthcare Sales Manager.

Erica is the founder of Trials 2 Triumph Coaching and Sisters Lifting Sisters. Trials 2 Triumph utilizes her 15+ years of professional and entrepreneurial experience to assist women seeking to find their purpose, establish a nonprofit, establish and market a business, or rise in their professional career. Sisters Lifting Sisters, non-profit organization, focuses on empowering women and children by bridging the gap between those who need assistance and their local resources. In January 2016, Erica launched SHERO Magazine, a publication highlighting women who are truly giving back to their communities. Shero salutes the silent community warriors who often go unrecognized and highlights women authors, health & wellness, fashion and coaching tips.

Throughout her philanthropic endeavors, family remains first! Erica enjoys traveling and spending time with her loving husband and business partner, Jonathan Green and 11-year-old daughter, Camryn Green.

To learn more about Erica visit, www.ericaperrygreen.com.

FELICIA A. GARRETT
Unmistakably Unstoppable

Most days I found myself mentally floating between the R&B songs, Superwoman or Every Woman. In one breath, I was belting out *"I'm not your superwoman"* and in the next breath I was declaring *"I'm every woman!"* Then, it just melted down to *"Precious Lord, take my hand."* Between family, church, work, business, and friends, I had my hands full. At any given moment, I would easily find myself running, almost flying, as if I truly did have super powers. From place to place and situation to situation, I was always coming in to save the day. The pressure, mostly self-imposed, to have the answers, meet the needs or to simply be whatever I was needed to be by those who needed and depended on me the most was overwhelming. The amount of energy required to be everything to everyone at all times was ridiculous.

Honestly, it was also fulfilling, especially when I heard words of appreciation and gratitude or when I observed the difference in a situation that was enhanced by my assistance. Coupled with the inner desire to please people, always do a great job, be perfect or to have things done perfectly, to not leave things undone or have anyone within my reach have unmet needs was the wind beneath my cape and it kept me going, that is until I crashed and burned.

I knew I was not alone. There were many other invisible cape wearing women all around me saving the day for anyone that crossed their paths in need of a *shero* that could solve the simple and complex issues of the moment while maintaining their daily lives with a smile on their face. The reality was, despite my best intentions, going through life wearing my cape was exhausting!

Yes, I know superwomen don't get tired, they don't get ill, they keep going despite the pain, hurts, heartaches, loss, setbacks, and life. So, what was wrong with me? I'd read Proverbs 31: 10-31 as Solomon's mother described the virtuous woman. She was the ultimate superwoman. She did it all and there was no mention of her having a need to rest.

She met the needs of her husband, children, and the poor. She made clothing, sold and bought land according to her needs, planted in the vineyard and represented her husband so well, that he was known among the elders. If she could do all that, what in the world was wrong with me? Why was I exhausted, with pains all over my body, irritable, agitated, easily frustrated, sad, feeling like a hamster on a wheel, confessing I was tired more than blessed, and just feeling like I wanted to buy a one way ticket to anywhere that I would not be known and escape for a season or two?

Those were the things I prayed for. I asked God to bless me with a family, a home, my job, opportunities to serve in ministry, options to work in my community, growth within my career, and the ability to help others live healthy lives. In retrospect, it took a lot of prayer, meditation, studying God's word, and a few crashes to realize I was not meant to do all of those things within my own strength and power. I was not meant to wear a cape or be a superwoman in life to anyone. I was designed and purposed to be a daughter to the king of kings, to seek him in all things and to rely on him for strength, guidance and wisdom.

I know, this sounded like a cop-out for me to step down from my responsibilities or to not accept ownership for things I desired. Believe me, I had that talk with myself many times. The truth was, I found out being a cape wearing superhuman in life was killing me. It was draining me of energy I needed to pursue my purpose and to be the woman I now know God designed for me to be.

I was suffering physically, mentally, emotionally, and spiritually as I struggled to do it all while doing it all. The pressure and strain was taking a toll on my health and my happiness. Although I was doing things I loved, the love of doing them was overshadowed by the reality that I had so much to do. I found myself physically present, but mentally my mind was miles away preparing for the next task or actually doing something else instead of being holistically present in the current moment. Yet, this was the expectation of me in society.

Multi-tasking was a required skill and the more I could do at one time, the more marketable I was in many areas of life. Why would I want, or even need, to take off my cape? What would it benefit me? Would I gain a few more hours of sleep? Maybe a few less activities on my daily task list? Maybe, I would gain the peace of mind I so desired or the opportunity to become unstoppable in all that I set out to do by simply not trying to fix everything for everyone, taking on less, being more present, and doing things that I found fulfilling?

I knew I had to make a change when my oldest daughter had a "come to Jesus" with me about my attitude and

Thanksgiving dinner. I loved Thanksgiving. It was my favorite holiday. I loved fellowship with family and friends, food, and I loved to cook and share those things I cooked with my loved ones.

That particular Thanksgiving, I had worked four ten-hour overnight shifts the week leading up to Thanksgiving. My plate was full with additional activities I just could not forfeit. I participated in a basket giveaway and several other church activities, held private client appointments and had school activities with my kids. Needless to say, a sister was done. I, then, came home the morning of Thanksgiving and proceeded to finish cooking my families' dinner without asking for help. Because I was worn out, unfocused, and not my best self, dinner was bearable, not my normal and it was not good. I was snappy, agitated, irritable, and tired for weeks prior to the holiday just from trying to do it all.

Concerned, my daughter shared that she missed me; the encouraging, optimistic, fun, and available me. She missed hearing me laugh and seeing me happy. She shared that I looked drained and she asked that I never cook a Thanksgiving dinner like that ever again in my life! I honestly did not realize that everything had changed so much in me. Of course, I presented shocked with her confrontation but beneath the surface, I knew it was truth. However, just to make sure I got the message, she included reinforcements from her siblings and my sister. They all shared similar sentiments; I needed to get it together and slow down. My husband had been sharing similar concerns that went unacknowledged. It took my family and my body to make me realize it was time to take off my cape.

Unfortunately, I forgot, as many women often do, that the most important person I needed to nurture, care for, and be there for was myself. To be there for others, I needed to be full and overflowing with all that I was giving away. If not, mood changes, loss of motivation, unhappiness and utter burnout occurred and occurred often. Overtime, with a decreased awareness and lack of attention to my own needs, the weight of the cape became unbearable, and the expectations began to be a burden.

It took literal emotional crashes and physical health concerns to make me recognize the importance of self-care. The experience taught me a very valuable lesson and brought to reality a saying I often heard as a child from my grandmother's women's circle; "you cannot serve from an empty vessel".

Although unintentional, my vessel was empty. Most of the time, I was existing solely on fumes. I moved from one thing to another, flying to the rescue in my cape, getting things done all the while mustering up enough energy in the moment to fully engage only to fall apart as soon as I was alone. My prayers were more so pleas for strength from task to task, as I no longer viewed things in any other manner than being a task to complete and check off my list of things to do. That included church, family outings and the limited times I would be with friends. Everything had become a task. Until that come to Jesus wakeup call that made me surrender and truly seek God for peace.

I was a believer, a worshiper, a mother, a wife, active with charities, a worker in the community, a leader on my job, and a leader in my church. I was not doing evil things so why didn't I have peace? It was simple, because I was neglecting to take care of myself.

That's it? Self-care, really? It seemed so simple yet so complex all at the same time. It made so much sense it was confusing. I took care of myself, didn't I? I bathed, kept my hair and nails nice, my clothing was always clean and appropriate, and I tried to remember to eat regularly. Exercise was another story, but, for the most part, I took pretty good care of myself. So, it didn't make sense that I needed to do more to feel better.

The error was in my thought process about self-care being selfish when, in actuality, self-care was self-preservation. I'm not talking about spa days, although those are nice, I'm talking about daily doses of self-care that nourish the mind, body and soul. In order to indulge in this new-found need, I first had to take off the cape. It wasn't easy but it was truly worth it and added a value to my life that was priceless. Here are a few things that helped me take off my cape.

"I have always believed that women hold this world together with their love, passion, inspiration, hard work, vision and willingness to help others. Yet, increased responsibility in both our personal and professional lives — to become "superwomen" — is taking a devastating toll on our health and happiness." ~ Simin Hashemizaden

Taking off my cape was a process of surrender, re-evaluation, nourishing, and learning how to say no. My prayer life was no longer desperate pleas for strength. It transitioned into daily conversations with my heavenly father. I sought His direction and guidance for my day and communicated my needs and desires to Him. I surrendered my will to His will. I read a daily devotion or scripture that gave me wisdom and understanding. For me, surrender was necessary multiple times during the day, especially when I found myself feeling anxious to do more.

I took an honest self-evaluation of my motives and compared them to my purpose. I had to acknowledge that in some areas I desired to help were not out of a pure heart. In some instances, my desire to help others was an effort to avoid doing some work on myself or to avoid something particularly challenging for me.

I overcame the struggle I had with saying no. I can't explain the struggle other than to say it seemed rude and uncaring. However, I found myself saying yes very often then dreading the task as it approached because I had not fully considered the cost of my yes. The cost was not about money; this cost was my time and energy. I had to learn that time was non-refundable and personal energy was a hot commodity.

To increase my energy and peace I had to increase my self-nourishment. It required gaining an understanding of what fueled me and challenging myself to identify things that did not require other people. Increasing my physical activity, rest, sleep, journaling, reading, and time alone were all things I found that fueled me. Incorporating them into my day was challenging but without them I was not able to give or be my best me.

Taking off the cape allowed me to gain a level of peace that I thought was unachievable. My level of personal and professional success has increased because I've learned balance. That was the secret of the Proverbs 31 Woman. Now, I'm a better person; a better woman. In my pursuit to accomplish my dreams and achieve my goals it was imperative that I not only take the cape off but that I keep it off. It's hard to be an unstoppable woman when you are stopping yourself. I finally realized (1) I can't be everything to everyone, (2) I'm not perfect and it's okay not to be, and (3) I am not superwoman nor am I every woman…I'm just one woman, an imperfect woman striving to be all that God desires me to be; Unmistakably Unstoppable!

About Felicia

Felicia A. Garrett is mother, wife, licensed professional counselor, speaker, mentor and instructor. She is the owner of Renewed Perspectives Counseling and Consulting Services, LLC. She enjoys helping women, couples and young adult's process through life's challenges and transitions to become their best self. Her life joys are her family, the opportunity to experience God's unconditional love daily and the privilege to share it with others.

To learn more about Felicia visit,
www. renewedperspectives.info.

KAREN BONNER
Unconditionally Unstoppable

There are no problems in life, only opportunities to grow us to our next level. This was the motto I lived by, however, my journey there wasn't easy. At first, I was only doing enough to get by and stay under the radar of life's curve balls. However, no matter how hard I tried they seemed to always find me. My inward thoughts of who I was displayed outwardly through impulsive actions that negatively affected me. I often thought I was invincible, only to be proven wrong by life's challenges. I was a single parent constantly attracting abusive relationships and stuck in poverty. My relationship with God was old and stale. I felt my voice was muted and I was in constant struggle with a chaotic life that belonged to me. My skin had been tattooed with layers of hurt, shame, and despair. I often wondered what I did to deserve such a life of turmoil and strain. I wanted to fight back but how could I fight and with what?

My body lay lifeless in the dark, cold, rat infested alley where the attacker dumped me after I was raped. My face and body were badly bruised and my canary yellow shorts were soaked in blood. I just knew my body would not be found. I was in the jaws of death. I felt my life leaving my body. Though I was not physically speaking, my heart was! Inside I was crying out to God. At that moment, I discovered the power of the name of Jesus; the life sustaining power.

I never reported my assault to any authorities because I was ashamed. I felt it was my fault; I was in the wrong place. I was only nineteen years old. I still needed protecting. I beat myself up for years because of this. But I didn't heal properly from the wound. The alley experience was forever embedded in my memory bank shaping how I loved myself, my children, and others. Though I was raised in the church and my parents were both ministers, it was this experience that really forged my relationship with God. Even in the horrors of this tragedy though, I still didn't give my life completely to Him! I continued to make unhealthy choices concerning finances, parenting, and love relationships.

I was broken. Some would say I was damaged goods but I refused to believe that "there was something wrong with me". However, years passed and it was evident I wasn't moving in the right direction. In my fragmented state, I met a man who swept me off my feet. He was charming and gentle. I thought, just the medicine I needed to help me move on with my life. How wrong I was!

We met in the summer of 2006 and married in the December of that same year. I thought I was ready for a new life with a man I loved and trusted. I felt this *had* to be better than what I had become used to. Everything was going great until I posted our wedding pictures on MySpace®. Shortly after posting, I received a message from a fourteen-year-old girl, stating that the picture of the man I posted as my husband was her father and he was still married to her mother! I was blown away. When I didn't think it couldn't get any worse, my interrogation of him finally revealed the truth; he was married with five children who lived in another state! Once we married, he never went back to them. Immediately, I was overtaken with hurt, shame, and utter disgust at what he had done. There was no way to fix this.

Shortly after our confrontation, I came home to find him gone with everything including my car. I felt like I had been raped all over again and every ounce of dignity I had gained was lost in that selfish act. I remembering crying out to God to save me. The hurt and embarrassment was far too much for me to bear! Life was suffocating me and I had no energy left to fight! The tools I thought I learned were powerless with no real relationship with God. My prayers were empty and I went to church service after service burdened. I'd heard *"take your problems to the altar and leave them there"* but I didn't actually know *how* to leave them. So, I went burdened and I left the same way I went.

A couple of years passed and time lessened the crying but the residue of life tragedies was still hidden in my heart. My annulment had just been finalized and I was attempting to piece my life back together but the financial devastation it created was too difficult to overcome. Despondent, I filled out the paper work that declared myself and my four children homeless. Knowing the weight of what state we were all in, we all sat and cried together. There was no extended family or friends to come to my rescue. There was no one to give me encouraging words. However, the look in my children's eyes sparked the energy to fight. I told them, *"Never look like what*

WAKE. PRAY. SLAY: A Woman's Guide to Being Unstoppable

you are going through and when life throws you a curve ball, it's ok to cry, but get back in the game and play to win!"

I was left scarred by my failed marriage that left me hardened and closed to love. The fiery anger that grew within me fueled a fire that seemingly would not be kindled. I displayed excitement for life publicly but, behind closed doors, I fought, cursed, and screamed every moment that I could. My makeup was on point, my hair was slayed but, inside, my soul was torn. Blow after blow, I was spiraling out of control. I knew I needed to slow down, but I was caught up somehow in a violent whirlwind that refused to release me from its grip. So, I prayed another rescue prayer, relying on God to lead me to safe housing. He proved to be faithful, yet again, and never left us.

Determined not to be beaten by life, I pooled all my focus and energy on the gifts God had given me. I had what my family needed to survive literally right in the palm of my hands. I decided I didn't want to just survive anymore, I wanted to thrive. Using my gift of cosmetology, I purchased a salon. *"I have $35.00 and passion,"* I confidently told the former owner. It literally felt like I had $35,000! Dedicated and passionate about being in this new place, I was determined not to fail. Becoming a salon owner was one of the proudest moments of my life. *She Salon* was my pride and joy. I had been through so many trials, I felt like this was my reward for enduring the hardness and passing the test. I could finally see the light.

As with any start up business, there were challenges and days I had to make decisions between business and home; whether I should buy product or buy groceries. There were many days that I wanted to give up but I had to remember just how far the Lord had brought me. The fact that my children were onlookers, giving up was a thought that I quickly dismissed. Eventually, the good days outweighed the bad days and I was in a new place mentally, spiritually and emotionally. I paid off $20,000 debt within nine months. Looking back on this time of my life, I can see that God was shifting me for the life that I now live.

Because I finally allowed the healing to take place in my life, I was allowed a beautiful soul that came into it and, with great care and compassion, he gently helped with the healing process. He was my friend first, moving at, what would be considered by most, an unusually slow pace, but he was a man that thought things through before acting swiftly. He was the exact prescription I needed in my life. He didn't have any characteristics of the other men I dated. His patience was phenomenal because the emotional wall I had built to guard my heart, body and soul was incredibly tall. Being with a woman that had been trampled so many times by my life circumstances, His love was cleansing, restorative, and sacrificial. I finally had someone in my life with the same mindset; a life partner who knew how to fight.

My relationship with God is awesome, I can, now, say that I truly have a relationship with Him that extends pass the walls of a building. It has become deeper and more meaningful. I fellowship with Him privately and corporately. My private worship time is the most precious and intimate time. He hears my heart and I hear His. There are days when I am challenged by my 4:30 a.m. wake up, but those are the times I need Him the most. I am confidently His daughter and I follow the leading of the Holy Spirit. I walk in love and seek to be non-judgmental daily, now, not overlooking my past, but remaining humbled by every opportunity that it has presented me. I am stronger and wiser now. I speak with Him often throughout my day. In the morning when I rise, I give thanks with a heart of gratitude. I meditate to hear what He has to say and I go into the world to be used by Him.

Wake, Pray, Slay is more than a catchy title for me, it is a lifestyle. I choose to live this way every day with continual effort and dynamic actions. I get things done! I am awakened and understand that no-thing gets completed if I am not at my best. Therefore, I have set in place daily rituals that assist with my well-being and they may help you too:

1. Affirmations spoken daily may counteract low self-esteem, self-doubt, and even fear. Practicing daily, affirmations combat negative feelings with positive self-talk throughout my day.

2. Forgiveness is key to unlocking the blessings to flow freely in your life. Begin with yourself and then others. Exercising daily forgiveness daily frees you to give yourself a pass when making mistakes and helps you to understand that you can start again.

3. Gratitude grows you. The more gratitude you display the greater increase in the amount of happiness you experience throughout your day. Focus on your abundantly blessed life and not on the negative aspects.

4. Journaling is important. It can be a point of reference to track your growth! Clarity is a

great benefit of journaling. Housing destructive thoughts, concerns, or ideas may cause you to act emotionally and impulsively.

5. Read. Gain knowledge about the things that interest you. Reading will help to expand your mind and motivate the change you desire to happen in life.

6. Eat well. Eating the right foods and staying hydrated during your day will also aid in giving you clarity, lessening headaches, and increasing your energy.

7. Connect with like-minded people that will sharpen you as you sharpen them! I explore new areas that allow me to be introduced to sharp and intelligent people.

For over a year now, I have been committed to living life to the fullest no matter what opportunities come. I realized my life could not change until my perception of the process changed. I am no longer the helpless victim awaiting rescue! I choose to be the rescuer of my own life; I wake, pray, slay, and I am Unconditionally Unstoppable!

About Karen

Karen Young Bonner is a native of Winston-Salem, North Carolina. She is a proud wife and mother of five. For over 18 years, Karen has been empowering women. Her efforts began in 1998 at North Carolina Correctional Institute for Women as she served as a Volunteer Clergy member through Kairos Prison Ministry.

Karen Young Bonner is the owner of Karen Bonner & Co., a Lifestyle Management Company that provides private coaching for individuals and groups. She is the founder of the See.Her.Evolve movement, and ALIVE Prayer and Share, unifying and connecting women with a community of like-minded individuals. Karen is a three-time Salon Owner, Master Stylist and Cosmetology Educator. She has helped numerous women discover their passion and start businesses. Karen is the co-founder of LovePack a marriage ministry focused on building marriages through intimate conversation.

To learn more about Karen visit, www.seeherevolvenow.com.

KIMBERLYNE ROUNDTREE
Fearlessly Unstoppable

The year 2008 was one to remember for me! My stepfather died on September 19th. My uncle died on September 26th. My mother died on November 14th... November 14th. Exactly eight years ago to the date I composed this piece, I was on a plane from Charlotte, North Carolina to San Jose, California with my husband of four years and my two-year old daughter. Although we were enjoying all that God had for us, I knew I didn't have much time left with my mother before she passed away. You see, seven years earlier my mom, Lula Briggs-Galloway (Google her) had been diagnosed with stage four lung cancer, but she was such a positive soul that unless she told you she had cancer, you would never have known. In fact, her relentless will to live was of such the doctors had never seen before.

Before we took off for California, I received a phone call from my cousin telling me that my mom wasn't doing well and that I should hurry home. My mother and I had a very special bond, you know the bond that allows you to sense things about the other even when they're not around. During the flight, I sat in the window seat next to my husband. About an hour into the flight, I looked out the window and felt my mom's presence so strongly that I fell asleep thinking about her. When I woke up, I awoke from a dream where I'd had a conversation with her. With no confirmation, other than what I felt deep down on the inside, I met my husband's gaze and said, "My mommy is gone."

Once we landed, I made the call. I was told, *"Just hurry up, Kimmie."* When we finally arrived at the house, I saw my aunt, my cousin, and a police officer standing on the porch. I don't remember the car stopping, I just remember leaping out of it. As I ran toward the house, I could feel my heart pounding in my chest. My aunt said, *"Go see your mom, Kim."* I paused briefly, knowing she had passed away, before I headed toward her room.

There she was, lying in bed, apparently asleep, but when I leaned down to kiss her, I noticed her skin was cool to the touch. I grabbed her and held her as close as I could, weeping like I had never wept before. I don't know how much time passed, but I remember the moment the coroner walked in the door. They told my family, *"Please have her daughter leave the room while we exit the house."* I didn't want to leave. I wanted to be with her for as long as I could.

I watched them roll my mother's body out of the house in a black body bag and I felt like everything in me was being rolled out right along with her. My mother gave birth only once - to me! Now I was having to figure out how I was going to live my life without her. She left explicit instructions regarding her memorial service. Since her body was to be cremated, I followed her wishes to the letter, leaving her ashes in a California vault right beside my grandmother.

I lost the only father I had ever known. Seven days later I lost my only living uncle. Then, less than two months later, I lost my mother. The losses happened so fast until I don't think I had a chance to grieve them properly. Most of the time, I wasn't even sure who I was crying for. I walked around for at least two years feeling numb.

During that time, I was unable to mention my mother's name or even listen to others talk about her. It took me nearly two years to return to California because I knew it would mean reopening the wound. When I finally did return to go through my mother's things in storage, I came across a handheld recorder. Curious, I pushed play and heard her voice. Shaken to the core, I dropped it and ran to my car. I wasn't coping well and I knew I needed professional counseling and medication.

Seeking therapeutic intervention was a challenge for me because I was told that Christians didn't take medication and should only rely on prayer. On two occasions, I considered suicide. I just didn't want to continue living without my mother. The first time, I kept it secret and didn't tell a soul. The second time, I shared it with my husband. I began to make-believe that my mother was alive and in California. I thought that would help, but when I desperately needed to talk with her, I would pick up the phone to call and then realize she wasn't there.

I didn't understand it then, but the root of my inability to release my grief was fear. After my mother died, I was suddenly fearful of everything. I feared not being good enough, not making enough money, dying prematurely, doing poorly in ministry, and the list goes on. My business partner gave me a Creflo Dollar CD called *The Many Faces of Fear*. I played it constantly for three straight months. It wasn't exactly new material. I used to speak the favor of God over my life and come against thoughts of fear and unbelief regularly, but when I got lost in depression, I was vulnerable and left myself open to the fear. I worried too much, meditated on the wrong things, and was generally over concerned about everything else in between. Once I renewed my mind with the truth, I took back the ground I gave to the enemy and began to speak life words. I started to believe and meditate on God's Word instead of my feelings and it worked! God's Word pulled me out of the horrible pit I was in and made me want to live again.

I started my own company in 2007 so it was in its infancy at the time my mother passed away. The reality is that when you're in a semi-depressed state, you do what you need to do to get through each day. We all have our own coping mechanisms and I had two things working in my favor; work and family. However, I found it far more challenging to interact with people because, at times, for no apparent reason, I would suddenly break down and cry. To combat my feelings, I spent as much time as I could with my daughter, Hannah. She brought me such great joy and reminded me a great deal of my mother.

For as long as I can remember, my mother was an entrepreneur. She owned her own business of one kind or another: hairdresser, paralegal, civic leader, museum owner, club owner, and real estate investor. Everything she did was to ensure I had a better life. I attended private school until my freshmen year of college when I attended a women's college in Los Angeles, CA. My mother made sure that I participated in extracurricular activities and she took me traveling a lot. When asked why she poured so much into me, she simply stated, *"My job is to make sure she is well cared-for."* And she did just that!

My father was murdered when I was a year old, so I don't remember him, but my mother made sure the money I received at my father's death was used for my benefit. I never wanted for anything for which I am very grateful. Yes, I lived a sheltered life but I wouldn't have it any other way. In time, my mother chose to marry her dear friend, Charles Galloway, to whom she was married until he died.

As strange as it may sound, my mother had always been proud of me, even though I'd made some bad choices. When I mentioned starting my own company, she said, *"It's about time. Now make it happen, Kimberlyne."* I heard those words echoing in my ear after she died and I worked tirelessly to make it happen just for her.

I worked tirelessly, day and night, pouring all my pent-up energy into my company so it would be the best it could be while grieving deeply. To get through most nights, I held my daughter in my arms. Holding on to her kept my spirit calm and made me quite happy. The Lord would often give me gentle reminders of His love for me. My daughter, Hannah, my husband, Steven, my friends, and family members all did their best to show their love in ways that gave me a reason to live.

I took the medication long enough to extricate myself

from the lowest place I'd ever known. Then, with the help of the Holy Spirit and professional help, gradually weaned myself off it. Once off the meds, there was an eight-year period I had no memory of. It was as if I had checked out of life as I'd known it.

I didn't realize that grieving was an active process of my transformation. I moved from the pain of mourning through the process of grieving. I learned how to honor the relationship I had with my mother and her memory by focusing on the positive things I loved. I developed a new identity and began to realize who I was in Christ and the purpose God had for my life despite the loss of my mother.

Until I began to write this, I didn't realize that it had been eight years since my mother passed away. It seemed like only yesterday, and as I look back I can't help but thank God for His resurrection, restoration, and regeneration power. He has given me a new beginning, as if I'm starting all over again. He can do that because He is God, and nothing is too hard for Him. I want to take this opportunity to praise Him and thank my family and friends for walking me through the valley of the shadow to the new dawn on the other side. In fact, when I realize that others have gone through it but didn't survive, I am profoundly grateful.

The Solace Group, the consulting company I started over ten years ago, has been a great source of income, and I thank God for strategically placing people in my life to move the company forward. This company will forever be my baby. But I believe God wants me to do more for Him. So, I will endeavor to do so as a merchant within the business mountain. Overcoming my trials pushed me toward greatness and allowed me to see that I am Fearlessly Unstoppable!

About Kimberlyne

Kimberlyne G. Roundtree's broad base of expertise gained throughout her years of experience enables her to fuse her passion for administration and her love for building organizational structure. A pro at working with organizational cultures of all sizes, Kim has perfected the art of examining an organization to aide in its transformation. She enjoys helping organizations move forward while experiencing greater outcomes. She is, also, adept at developing tools, processes, strategies, and structures that prompt cultural change. For over twenty-three years, Kim has worked in child welfare, school social work, mental health, foster care and the prison system. For six years, she co-owned four mental health facilities in Louisiana eventually selling to a major inpatient hospital.

Kim's natural gift of administration moved her to create Momentum; a consulting firm providing web based and onsite consulting services to organizations. Momentum strives to propel organizations forward by assessing their internal health, exposing blind spots and designing a plan that can be effectively executed. Momentum provides service in three areas – Business, Ministries and Events.

Kim is married to Steven Roundtree and they have four children: Hannah, Michael, Ashton and Phoenix, the family dog.

To learn more about Kimberlyne visit, www.momentum8.com.

LATASHA WILLIAMS
Purposely Unstoppable

I grew up in a house with my mom. She was an avid partier, always wore fancy dresses, and had lots of friends. My daddy never lived in our house but I knew him. Because of the lifestyle my parents chose to live, I didn't have the best of influences. By the time I was eight years old, both parents had full on drug addictions and like that my life began to change. It was on a slow spiral downhill and I was powerless to stop it.

I managed to keep my mom's addiction a secret from everyone at school. No one but the neighborhood drug pushers really knew she was hooked. Many days I would come home from school just in time to see them coming out of my house after they had sold my mom drugs. If I was driving my mom's car, they would roll and ask me if "I was straight" thinking I was my mom.

Growing up in this kind of environment as a teenager was kind of hard. I did different things to try to escape what was going on around me and in the neighborhood. Though it may not have been the best choice, I began to take an active interest in boys.

As a young girl, boys always seemed to make everything a little bit better. I found out the hard way that they didn't actually make everything better, they just provided a temporary distraction from the daily frustration and pain. At that time, though, that was all I needed.

By the time I registered for school at Cleveland State University, I was pregnant with my first child. I remember thinking, all this will be simple. I am a new mommy so I will sign up for welfare, get an apartment, go to class, find a part time job, and be "fly" all at the same time. It was so funny and foolish of me. Well, I did sign up for welfare. I did go to school. I did get an apartment but that was where my perfect plan fell apart.

I was in and out of college. Because my mind was all over the place, I often found myself in between jobs. The student loan refund checks helped boost me but working here and there sometimes was simply not enough. Thank God I had a grandmother who always supported my children and I financially, but there were times, even then, where I struggled. She helped me so much sometimes my pride wouldn't let me always go to her.

I was young, out in the world, doing what I had to do but I didn't always make the right choices. By the time I was nineteen, I was married with a little girl on the way. After we had our second child, I found out that my husband didn't want to be married anymore. How could this be? He was a man in the church and raised in the church. He seemed to have the right pedigree but he was lacking in the area of integrity.

We had many legal issues while married. We used credit cards and wrote checks to live...well we wrote bad checks, that is. We were both physically abusive to each other and after a time, we decided the best thing for us to do was to separate. So, I packed up my three children and tried to move on with my life but it proved to not be such an easy task. I just couldn't I let him go.

I allowed this man to come and go as he pleased because on paper, we were still married. He would come lay with me, play house with me and confuse my children...and I allowed it. Honestly, it felt good to be wanted and fulfilled but it also left me feeling a horrible mess every time he walked out the door. Eventually, I gain the strength to put an end to it. I had learned to self-medicate with men, though. So, the vicious cycle stopped with him, but it continued with the next man.

Now I had been with my husband since I was nineteen. By the time I got to my late twenties, I thought I would do better if I didn't choose "a man in the church". I was still hurting, trying my best to mask it, and I chose the next relationship looking to fill the void. I'm not sure what I expected but in the next relationship, I allowed some things that I should not have. I grew up in the church and I knew better, but for a few years I settled.

This man and I never lived together but he did have clothes in the bottom drawer (if you know what I mean). All the while I felt horrible because I was not living a life that was honorable in the eyes of God. Soon, that relationship came to an end but my life kept going. I was still a single mother with three children trying to figure things out to the best of my ability.

After that relationship, I was actually starting to get the hang of it. I'd started a wedding and event planning company and things were going pretty good. That is until my past reappeared. Remember the credit cards and bad checks I wrote? I thought I had gotten away with something and years later it came knocking at my door. I was in the fight of my life for five long months. I was in and out of court and I didn't and how it would turn out. The day of my court appearance, I just knew I was walking up out of there. The judge had other plans. He sentenced me to six months in prison and I almost lost my mind.

The seven days I was preparing to go to women's prison were the hardest seven days of my life. I refused to see my children as I didn't want them to see me that way. I was in the county jail ready to be shipped out but I wasn't going to go quietly. I did something most people would consider strange. Every night I asked the women if they wanted to pray. Some women wanted to, some didn't. It began with only a few women. Then, each night, more would join. The night before I was due to be shipped to the women's prison, I was cleaning up and sweeping. It was my night to do chores. The correctional officer said, "*You have court in the morning.*" I said, "*No, you must have the wrong person. I'm due to be shipped out in the morning.*" I had accepted the fact of having to serve the prison time. The officer then said, "*No, you're going to court in the morning.*" Not understanding but in my heart not believing her, I continued my task. After I finished cleaning up, I went to my area and prepared for bed. I did the old school roll-up-your-hair-with-some-toilet-tissue-and-grease and went to sleep. I wanted to be as presentable as I possibly could for the next morning.

The next morning, my name was called for court an hour before they usually call the women to be shipped out. Let me make this plain so you can understand what was happening. You didn't just go to court. They would call you and you would go downstairs. You were kept in a holding area for about four or five hours where you could eat breakfast and wait until your turn to go in front of the judge. At this point I was still confused about what was happening because I was expecting to be shipped to the women's prison.

Finally, my name was called and I was escorted to the court room to stand in front of the judge. This was the very judge who has sentenced me to serve six months. He looked at me said, "*I don't know why, but you are going home today.*" I turn around to see who had come to witness what was taking place in this court room. There was an attorney that was well known attorney standing beside my grandmother. I saw them shake hands and I turned back to face the judge. He, then, said to me, "*This is not the normal at all.*" He proceeded to explain that I was standing before him because he had received letters from people who had spoken on my behalf. He continued by saying there was one letter, in particular, that stood out the most for him. It was a letter from one of my daughters. The judge said the letter read, "*Bad people go to jail and my mommy is not bad*". Right then and there, the tears began to flow.

Dazed and in disbelief, I was escorted to the area where you wait to be released. Before I could go, they had to do a national background check which took some time, so I was taken back upstairs to my cell. When the ladies from my cell block saw me, they couldn't believe it. They were cheering for me and encouraging me. They stated emphatically that because I came in and prayed with them in spite of my situation, they were able to witness the miraculous power of God move in my life on that day. That was truly a moment I will never forget.

I forged lifelong relationships with a couple of women I met while in jail. One lady was involved in a ministry that helped reform women out of prison. It was such a joy for me to be a part of that ministry to be able to connect with women who, like myself, were not bad people but had just made some bad choices.

In the aftermath of my legal problems, my finances suffered greatly. The relationship I was in ended. I suffered through a couple of health issues and ended up losing my home but I had a peace in knowing that God was for me. Romans 8:31 says, *"What shall we then say to these things? If God is for us, who is against us?"*

I had the women's ministry for women out of prison and I was planning events but God began to tug at me to do more. In the basement of my home Women of Purpose was born. It began just like the Lord impressed upon my heart while I was locked up - with women coming together to pray.

I knew there were women who needed to know that there was a safe place to talk and that they could make it.

Not long after my life returned to a sense of normalcy, God restored back to me everything I had lost. I was blessed with another home and I was finally in a place where God could send me a man that would not only wed me, but be a father to my children and cover us in every way God designed for him to. We joined my three children and his two into a wonderfully blended family that we could nurture, love, and protect. The greatest pleasure of my life is knowing that everything I went through was not in vain. I didn't understand it then but I was simply being built to be Purposely Unstoppable!

About Latasha

Latasha is a native of Cleveland, Ohio. She is the owner of Twice as Nice Consign and Boutique where she delights in helping women obtain the finer things in life without spending an enormous amount of money. Latasha is a Certified Occupancy Specialist in the corporate arena, however, she has a strong passion for The Purposed Woman; which prompted her to found the women's organization Women of Purpose (W.O.P.) a group that understands that though we are not Jesus, we are His hands.

Latasha lives by two mottos:
"We should always have three friends in our lives-one who walks ahead who we look up to and follow; one who walks beside us, who is with us every step of our journey; and then, one who we reach back for and bring along after we've cleared the way." ~ Michelle Obama

"Over the years I have learned that what is important in a dress is the woman who is wearing it." ~ Yves Saint Laurent

To learn more about Latasha visit, www.womenofpurposeglobal.com.

REKETTA C. WRIGHT

MONICA LEWIS
Powerfully Unstoppable

I t was late summer. September, if I remember correctly. It was three o'clock in the morning and I was at home lying in bed anxiously tossing back and forth. Unable to sleep, I got up to check on my children; a beautiful five-year old boy and a seven-year old girl whom I loved with everything in me. I peeked into each room and briefly watched them sleep. I always found it intoxicating to watch them at peace, but when I headed back to my room I couldn't escape the feelings of dread that washed over me.

The reality of my situation plagued me night after night. I was haunted by feelings of betrayal, loneliness, and anger. I should have been laying, cuddled up next to my husband of one year. Instead, I lay there, once again, wondering whether he was in the arms of another woman. In my heart, I knew that's exactly where he was, but he would never admit to it. In fact, he continued to look me in the eye and lie to my face. Over and over he would say to me, *"I would never choose another woman over you"*. He was adamant that I was the one with the problem: the one who was making things up, the one with the issues, the one who was crazy.

So, there I was, once again. Shallow breath. In bed. Alone. Staring up at the ceiling. My mind was frantic. How could he do this to me! I did not deserve this. I began crying uncontrollably somehow feeling responsible for my situation. I chose him to partner with me in this thing called life, yet he didn't love me. He didn't respect me and all I could think about was why. Why couldn't I make him love me the way I needed to be loved? Why wasn't I pretty enough, sexy enough, or smart enough? Why wasn't I just ENOUGH? With no answers, I began to beg God to change me, to give me the right things to say to keep my husband at home. I begged Him to show me what to wear so he would choose me. I begged Him to give me the strength to endure. The more I begged, though, the angrier I became.

I called his cell phone again and again, but there was no answer. The third time I called, a woman answered the phone. I couldn't believe it. Every shred of dignity I had left slowly faded away as I begged her to speak to my husband.

Stunned and in disbelief, she put me on hold. I felt like I was going to die! My mind was racing, yet I couldn't stifle my curiosity. Who was she? What did she look like? Why did he keep choosing her instead of me? Then she hung up!

What was left of my sanity was gone with the click of that phone. I threw it across the room and spewed hatred at the only person I felt was truly responsible... GOD!

"God, how could you do this to me! I deserve better than this! I have been good to this MAN! I stay here night after night taking care of his children--helping them with their homework, cooking for them, and making sure they are taken care of while he repeatedly has sex with other women. He doesn't even have the decency to tell me the truth; that he just doesn't love me! Instead he lies and makes me feel like I am the crazy one. God, please give me the proof that I need to move on from this! Give me the proof to know whether I need to move on or to stay in peace," I cried.

Right then the door opened and my son came in the room. He heard me moving around the house and was concerned about me. He saw the tears that ran down my face and reached out to hug me. The closeness of our relationship was a blessing, a blessing that most could not understand. Sometimes I did not even understand it. I could only be happy that both of my husband's children loved me the way that they did. I was not the children's biological parent but the instant hurt I saw in his eyes when he saw me crying always let me know that it did not matter. He wanted to take my tears away from me. Trying to cover my pain, I kissed his forehead and sent him back to bed. Despite the way their father treated me, I wanted to protect them and their innocence. They didn't deserve this either.

At 7 a.m. the next morning, I awoke on the floor where I'd cried and prayed myself to sleep after my emotional rantings to God. I was so tired that I never even made it to the bed. I was stirred awake by the sound of someone moving around in the kitchen. Thinking it was one of the children, I entered to find my husband making something to eat as if nothing had happened.

When I walked into the room, he greeted me with a simple, *"Hello."* In my head, I was yelling, *"Are you serious! Hello! That's all you have to say to me!"* But the kids were sitting at the table, so I mustered up a very low and squeaky, *"hello,"* in return. As calmly as I could I continued, *"Where were you last night?"*

"You know where I was. Where do I always go on Friday nights? You act as if this is a new thing. I was with the boys. I always go out with the boys on Friday nights to watch the local football games."

"I didn't realize there were local football games that lasted all night. And that women actually attended those games with you and your friends," I replied.

"What do you mean? Women?"

"Like the woman who answered your phone after 3 a.m. last night."

"Girl you are crazy. That was my friend's cousin. She must have heard my phone ringing and answered it."

"Well, you never came to the phone."

"Because I knew you would be tripping. In fact, I could have gotten home a few hours ago but I decided to sleep in the parking lot at the grocery store up the street because I wanted to get some rest before I got home. I knew if I came home, I would hear your mouth and these lies you make up in your head."

Anger suddenly welled up inside me and tears streamed down my face. Unable to control my emotions, I ran out of the room so I wouldn't frighten the children.

I managed to pull myself together to help the kids get dressed. We had a full day of visiting family and friends so I stifled my feelings so I could get through the day. The whole time I felt like a fraud because our family had so many divisive secrets. We were simply living a lie. It wasn't long afterward I learned that there was no freedom in living a lie. God could not bless who we pretended to be.

Before leaving the house, I checked the mail. In it, I discovered my husband's monthly credit card statement. It had never come to the house before but there it was. I decided to run back into the house to open it. I slipped into the closet out of eye sight. I was shaking nervously because somehow I knew what I would find.

Viewing the statement, I noticed several purchases for hotel stays in a neighboring city. I knew I had not stayed in those places with him. My heart was broken but I was thankful that I finally had the proof I needed to call him on his lies. I wondered if this was God answering my prayers, but because I lacked confidence, I quickly dismissed it as a coincidence. Suddenly, I heard him call my name. *"Monica, let's go. My mom is expecting us."* I swallowed my pride, put the envelope in the top of my closet under a stack of jeans, and walked to the car.

On our way to visit his mom, we stopped at a gas station. Both he and one of the children were in a hurry to use the restroom. As he was unstrapping his son from the seat, he shoved his phone at me and asked me to hold it until he returned. I was instantly annoyed, yet I could not ignore the strong desire to look at his phone.

To my surprise, he had not taken the time to clear the screen. Coincidence #2? The numbers showed up in his phone as *70437625416485.* This was odd because there are only ten digits in phone numbers. Then it hit me. The last four digits were the code to his voicemail! I was speechless! It couldn't actually be this easy.

Frantically, I committed the numbers to memory before he returned. This had to be God's miraculous answer. I had asked for proof in my time of need, and He answered my prayer. This time I knew it was not a coincidence. God was showing His love. I asked and the proof was given.

During the next few days, similar incidents occurred repeatedly as God revealed unequivocal evidence that the man who promised to love me unconditionally was not who God called him to be! I was hurt but thankful at the same time. In fact, it opened my eyes to a side of God's character I had never experienced before. I knew that if God loved me enough to speak to me at my lowest and ugliest moments, He must see me differently than I saw myself. At that moment, I realized that He saw the beauty inside me even when I didn't see it. And if that was so, He also believed in my potential for great things.

My love for God grew exponentially in the days following. I began to look for evidence of Him in ordinary moments in the still of the day. God gave me the answers to my most burning questions in the most unexpected places; the words of a song, in the title of a movie, and even during a conversation with a friend. This new perspective of God changed everything, even the way I saw myself. My thoughts, that were once rooted in betrayal, insecurity, mistrust and self-hatred rose to thoughts of confidence, love, and the awesome possibilities of God. If the Spirit of God was within me as God's Word said it was, I could even believe that all things were possible.

Six months passed and I finally mustered up the courage to leave my husband. From that moment on, I committed myself to a new way of thinking and living in boldness. I continued to be thankful for God's incredible blessings. Every night before going to bed I listed all the wonderful things He had done in my life that day. When I woke the next morning, I would say, *"Thank you, God for loving me enough to…"* and I would list aloud each thing He had done the day before. Then I ended with, *"Thank you, God, for doing all those things and what you're going to do in my life today in a big way!"* This way of thinking became my source of power.

I called that exercise the Power Source Challenge and shared it with anyone I thought might benefit from a different way of thinking and a stronger spiritual relationship with God because it works. I've seen the changes and evidence in my own life as well as the lives of others. My inner man gained strength and my sense of self-worth grew to where I saw myself as whole and complete, because of the Holy Spirit in me.

I went from losing my husband, kids, my car to repossession, and making less than $38,000 a year to a successful entrepreneur who eventually sold a thriving business for seven figures. Now, I am in love with an awesome man who treats me with so much love and respect.

I have a beautiful daughter whom I pour love into every chance that I can get. My life has totally changed. I know that these accomplishments would not have been possible at the place where I was ten years ago. My thoughts and beliefs were deep-rooted in sinking sand. I did not love myself nor did I believe in the possibility of God working through me.

If you see yourself in my journey, I pray that it will help you analyze the source of your thoughts, the power of your beliefs, and the anchor of your faith. If your focus is not rooted in strength and unlimited possibilities, then you are living far beneath the life Christ has called you to. Let me assure you that if you feel inadequate and desperate, your feelings are deceiving you. The truth is that you are enough, and you can do all things with God working through you! Just make a small change today. Go through the Power Source Challenge. Step into a different mindset—a different expectation so that you, too, can be Powerfully Unstoppable.

About Monica

Monica Lewis is an entrepreneur, author and Power Alignment Coach. In 2006, Monica co-founded, The Solace Group, a consulting firm dedicated to helping mental health organizations in the areas of expansion, operations and programming. The Solace Group grew to become a beacon of leadership in the Mental Health Industry, consulting with hundreds of organizations all over the country. In 2010, The Solace Group decided to put the theory to practice to co-launch a brick and mortar Mental Health Clinic. Five years later, Monica and her partners sold the clinic for seven figures - an extremely rare feat in the Mental Health industry.

Monica is now the CEO and founder of Source Thought and Master Coach at Not Just Weight. Source Thought is a motivational and inspirational company that provides personal development, business coaching and products dedicated to spiritual growth and lifelong learning. Not Just Weight is a wellness program that combines the principles of Naturopathic Medicine, Lifestyle Medicine and Mindset to promote an easy transition into a healthier life.

Monica overcame an impoverished and unstable childhood with a drug abusing parent to owning and consulting for million dollar organizations. Her escape from a tumultuous past to business and personal success is what drives her desires to teach others to become their own change agents. Monica's overall mission, no matter the platform, is helping people see the grandest vision of themselves, then holding them accountable to realize it.

To learn more about Monica visit, www.iamsourcethought.com or www.lifestyle-clinic.com.

NATROSHA MILLER
Undauntedly Unstoppable

It was only a few years ago that I was trying to decide whether to give up on my miserable life or finally accept the call that God had placed on my life. I could never have imagined myself, a shy, small town, southern girl of Mississippi, an inspiration to women of faith across the globe. I often found myself wondering why God had chosen me; at that time, a cold-hearted, broken spirited woman to lead an inspiring, positive sisterhood community. God, knowing my exact thoughts, revealed to me later the reason why... to discover my purpose and to heal through the process. As my late great grandmother used to say, God works in mysterious ways. I didn't quite grasp the full understanding of the true meaning of that concept until I became a born again Christian.

I nearly lost my mind trying to live a life without a relationship with God. As I was experiencing the lows of my life, I often felt hopeless of tomorrow's promises, frustrated with meaningless relationships, and unloved by the people whom I cared for the most. I was depressed, disheartened, and discouraged to say the least.

Growing up, I had always been a very reserved yet observant person. Some people may have described me as a private person who mostly kept to herself. Nevertheless, I publicly declared my belief in Christ at the age of six. I was actively involved in church throughout my childhood. I knew that Jesus loved me and I loved Him. However, as a teen I found myself questioning God about His presence in my troubled life. I remember wondering what was the purpose of my life and how I could positively impact someone else's life. I questioned if I was worthy of making a difference in the world where I lived in poverty, surrounded by negative people and situations often witnessing family abuse.

In my early twenties, life caught me by surprise. I relocated from Jackson, Mississippi to Atlanta, Georgia for a change in my environment and to pursue a long-term career opportunity. Like most twenty-somethings, my life was very busy. I decided to focus on continuing my education at a private university in hopes of obtaining a business's degree in three years while working full time. After enduring the many hardships and struggles of my past, I was very determined to make a great life for myself and for those I loved. I knew success had my name written on it. It spelled out in unique pattern of letters: N-A-T-R-O-S-H-A!

When I married, I felt my life was flourishing beyond my dreams. What else could I possible desire, right? Despite what I "felt" during that period, life had proven to be better than I could have ever imagined. It was the evil, untruthful devil who tricked me into believing more of him and less of God. Nevertheless, I disobeyed God because the enemy had already convinced me that his plans for my life were better than God's plan. I made the wrong deal with the devil and lived in hell on earth for years because of it.

My marriage began to crumble and my perfect world along with it. I, soon, faced life alone and struggled to take care of myself as a single woman again. Though I tried desperately to put out the fires in my life, the smoke stains displayed boldly as a constant reminder of my disobedience to God. I, like most people, was afraid to admit anger with God over my life circumstances. Sadly, during that time I even blamed God for allowing my marriage to fail, my broken heartedness, the painful bruises on my body, and my public humiliation. Instead, I allowed the guilt of displeasing God to negatively impact my daily life and prevent me from being healed from the brokenness and disappointment. *"He heals the brokenhearted and binds up their wounds,"* Psalms 147:3.

I quickly discovered the decision to direct my own path for my life without God was my biggest mistake. Soon after, I was diagnosed with clinical depression. I was identified with a "major depressive disorder." There were days I wanted to hide out under the covers until the storms passed. I often felt hopeless about the future of my life. I battled thoughts of suicide planted by the enemy. Depression had me so down, I wanted to give up and literally throw in the towel. I felt my life was hopeless and there was no way out.

For years, I dealt with the depression and kept it a secret from everyone, including my family. Being the private person I was, I pretended to live a happy life but in reality, I suffered alone. I hid my mental issues from my family because I did not want my character to be judged by people who sought me for advice. In their eyes, I was a strong, independent, woman of God who had it all together. They couldn't know that I no longer made God first priority in my life. I couldn't tell them the guilt I carried being in a backslidden state. I cared too much about what people thought about me at that time. So, it was important for me to keep up the façade rather than expose the real me.

During those difficult times, I rarely attended Sunday church service. Eventually, I stopped praying to God altogether. I didn't believe God would forgive me and give me another chance to make a difference. I remember how each day became darker and the nights were lonelier during my untreated depression. I was frustrated yet I still couldn't muster up the strength to call on the Lord Jesus Christ. Every time I took one step forward, in despair, I found myself taking three steps backwards. The only thing that kept my focus, was completing my bachelor's degree in business management.

Late nights, unable to sleep with suicidal thoughts racing through my head. I often planned my funeral in my mind. Instead of planning to live, sadly the devil had me planning to die. But I was tired of pretending to be someone I was not anymore. One night crying, I went inside my dark bedroom closet. With the door barely open, I thought to just lay there until someone discovered my body and rolled me out in a hearse. The devil had me feeling like no one cared if I lived or died. That night, I found the true meaning of my late great-grandmother's quote "God works in mysterious ways" for myself.

I had a dog named Cassidy that I'd had for more than twelve years. He was a special dog. Unlike most dogs who played with toys, ran around the house, and barked if some unknown person entered the house, Cassidy was just the opposite. He was a sweet and quiet dog. He kept to himself unless he was eating his food. While I was crying my eyes out in the closet, I felt something rub against me. Startled, I immediately stopped crying and looked up to see Cassidy, who had somehow found me in the dark closet, licking on me. Someone who doesn't know how dogs show love wouldn't understand. For me, it was God's way of reassuring me that someone did need and care about me.   God used Cassidy to save me that night. Immediately, in that moment, I cried out to God like I had never cried out before. With tears falling down my face into the early hours of the morning, I prayed a prayer of repentance and got back in right relationship with the Lord. I poured out to God of my unclean heart and asked Him to create in me a clean heart and renew a steadfast spirt within me (Psalm 51:10).

During the process of my spiritual healing, God revealed to me my life's purpose and I was ready to try it His way. In my vulnerability, I surrendered solely to Him and allowed Him full access to my life. A message from T.D. Jakes entitled "Short Changed" especially ministered to me during that time. Everything I had gone through in the past years; He spoke on it. Bishop Jakes talked about the type of feelings I had that no one else knew but God. I never wept during a sermon of its entirety like I did when I heard that one. I embraced the fact that just because I felt I had been short changed in life, I was not cast down nor had I been forsaken. I was walking in my season of restoration. I was rebuilt, renewed, and restored.

From that moment forward, I shifted all my attention toward honoring God. He gave me the strength and courage to pursue my purpose, literally saved me from depression, and birthed a ministry from my deepest misery to inspire women across the globe. I am greater than depression because of God.

When you feel negative thoughts surfacing, fight back with God's word. *"He giveth power to the faint; and to them that have no might he increaseth strength. Even the youths shall faint and be weary, and the young men shall utterly fall: But they that wait upon the Lord shall renew their strength; they shall mount up with wings as eagles; they shall run, and not be weary; and they shall walk, and not faint"* Isaiah 40:29-31. Despite the challenges you may encounter, seek God for guidance and clarity in your life especially when making decisions. Always listen to Him and know you, too, are greater than depression because you are Unstoppable!

About Natrosha

Natrosha Miller is the Founding Visionary of the growing, inspiring Love Thy Sistahs Ministry, where she serves like-minded women of faith across the globe. She is also the creator of the "I Am My Sistah's Champion" movement that encourages women to share their powerful testimony.

Natrosha is originally from a small town of Mississippi, now she resides in the suburbs of Hampton, Georgia. She obtained her Bachelor's degree at Strayer University where she majored in Business Administration with a minor concentration in Human Resource Management.

Today, Natrosha's purpose and passion lies in helping women along their spiritual journey through words of inspiration and leadership.

To learn more about Natrosha visit, www.lovethysistahs.com.

RONKEYUNA GREEN
Triumphantly Unstoppable

*S*he is clothed with strength and dignity and she laughs without fear of the future" Proverbs 31:25, **NLT**. However, fear of the future is always what I had. Matriculating through grade school, all one looks forward to is senior year! Whether its high school or college, when one makes it to their senior year that means that they have completed the necessary requirements in order to move forward.

In elementary school, the teacher asked the big question, *"What do you want to be when you grow up?"* They, then, followed that question up with, *"Where you see yourself in the next five or ten years?"* I pondered those questions over and over and immediately answered without hesitation. I was overly confident that it was going to happen just like I planned.

When you're young, it never crosses your mind that even though you know what you want to become and even set goals to facilitate a favorable outcome, it doesn't always work out like you plan.

Looking back for me, every summer in grade school I spent in summer school. I had either failed a subject completely or didn't pass the standardized test required to pass to the next grade level. While my peers were extremely excited about their summer breaks, talking about what they were going to do with their families, and how much fun they were going to have, I was sad knowing that I would spend my summer months in summer school just so I could be promoted to the next grade. I also felt the sting of parents having to find money to pay for summer school. It was a vicious cycle that continued year after year until the year my dad refused to pay. He thought it would be best if, that year, I was held back to repeat the school year. He was adamant that he didn't have money to keep giving me to go to summer school and he felt like had I completed the work I should have while I was in school, we wouldn't be having that conversation. I mean, I couldn't blame him.

My mom always told me that I could do better. She recognized that I was just complacent and, honestly, I was. After repeatedly failing grades and going back and forth to summer school, I felt like a failure within myself and inferior to my peers (you know kids can be cruel). So, I developed the attitude that a C grade or a D grade was fine with me. It was still passing. My mother, however, wasn't going to let that fly!! She always encouraged me that I could accomplish anything I put my mind to.

When my father refused to pay for summer school, my mother just couldn't bear the thought of me being left behind. She sold pictures off our walls, did hair, and borrowed money to ensure that, one more year, I could go to summer school. I knew that was the last straw at that point because even she was getting tired of trying to save me.

By the time I made it to Junior High School, I started to take my education seriously. Because I hadn't applied myself earlier, later concepts became difficult to grasp. Math was one of those subjects. However, it didn't help me learn when I had to endure the teacher that was supposed to be my help, call me stupid or dumb. It was bad enough I already felt substandard to the other kids because I didn't comprehend like they did. The older I became and failed at something, those words always replayed in my mind. I would go home and literally cry myself to sleep asking, *"God, why me? Why can't I be this way or that way?"*

I experienced depression at an early age. At the time, I didn't know it was depression, I just knew I was sad all the time and suppressed a lot of things. I laughed and smiled to cover up the hurt and pain that I felt on the inside. Although I grew up in the church and knew God, it didn't stop the suicidal thoughts from coming. I questioned God numerous times about my life. I wondered what my purpose was in the world. I knew I wanted more out of life and didn't want to grow up struggling, but I wanted to be successful and wasn't quite sure if I could be.

I was extremely excited to make it to my senior year in high school. However, what I thought was going to be the best year of my life somehow ended up being the worst year I could have ever imagined. In order to graduate, juniors and seniors had to pass a standardized test (GEE – Graduation Exit Exam). Students were required to pass all four parts of the exam. Despite my best efforts, I passed only two parts of the exam and had to retake two parts. My grades were good but not passing the GEE ensured that I couldn't graduate. Grasping at what ounce of energy I had left, I was able to take the test once more, but again, I failed. I remember telling my best friend that I wasn't going to come see her graduate and congratulated her on her accomplishments. I told her it would be too painful to sit in the audience and watch her, along with all my classmates, walk across the stage knowing that I was supposed to be there walking with them. I managed to swallow my pride, though, and attend the graduation. That was, by far, the hardest thing I ever had to do.

Somehow, not graduating, I felt robbed. It was something I prayed for so long. I didn't realize I was praying amiss. Asking God to give me the desires of my heart left me questioning myself and trying to figure out what I had done wrong. I was confused I didn't know what to think or what to do. My desire to pray or seek the face of God drastically declined. I felt He had forsaken me. However, the more mature I became I began to understand how the power of prayer worked in relation to a strong relationship with God. I ditched my pity party and focused on going after Him wholeheartedly. I got back up, dusted myself off, and went after my dreams and aspirations.

I didn't allow my setback to deter me and I applied for school at a local junior college. I was so excited about my new journey. I always wanted to be a social worker, so that was the plan. One day on my way to class, God took me back to a conversation I had with an old classmate of mine when I was in high school. We were discussing our dreams, our goals, and what we wanted to do after we graduated. I was very sheltered growing up in that all I knew was church, home, and school. So of course, like any other young adult, I couldn't wait to get out of my parents' house so I could experience life on my own. I began planning my life by not once asking God what His plan for my life was. *"For I know the plans I have for you," declares the Lord, "plans to prosper you and not to harm you, plans to give you hope and a future"* Jeremiah 29:11, **NIV**.

After taking the courses I needed to take at the junior college, I was able to transfer to a four-year college; Grambling State University. I always wanted to attend an HBCU. I was working a full-time job and going to school full time. I wasn't balancing the job well with class so I was called in the office by management and given options concerning my job. Either I had to drop school or drop down from my full-time position to part time. There again, reality met me head on and I had to make a decision about the life I wanted to live. I definitely wasn't about to stop going to school. I had made it too far with great results and I wasn't about to jeopardize that.

Trusting in the Lord, I took a leap of faith and dropped down to part time. I didn't know how I was going to take care of my responsibilities. Working part time turned into hardly working no hours at all. However, God made a way. My checks were just enough to tithe and pay whatever bill was due that month. I didn't have extra money left to shop but my necessities were met. God was a provider and He did just what He said He would do. I had no other choice but to trust him. *"And this same God who takes care of me will supply all your needs from his glorious riches, which have been given to us in Christ*

Jesus" Philippians 4:19, **NLT**.

I went from working full time to working two part-time jobs with school full time. Talk about self-determination. It was tough getting off work at 7 a.m. and driving to my 8 a.m. class thirty-five miles away. Many mornings, my mind and my body were so tired that they began to shut down on me. Driving, I began to drift over in the other lane of oncoming traffic with eighteen-wheeler trucks behind. God had his angels encamped all around me and I had no accident. God truly had me covered. It was nothing but His hand of protection over my life and Him giving me the strength and courage to endure. I was determined to reach my goal and wasn't going to let anyone or anything stop me. I knew that I was destined for greatness. Nothing in my life came easy so my motto became, 'Work hard now, play hard later'.

Though I had many crying days, I survived. Lots of prayer and fasting allowed me to, once again, achieve senior status. This time graduation is sure with a promising career to follow in the field that I always desired. Our timing is not God's timing but in due time it will come to pass. My story is still being written and the best is yet to come. Every day, I wake, pray, and slay because I am Triumphantly Unstoppable!

About Ronkeyuna

Ronkeyuna Green is a native of Monroe, Louisiana. There, she serves faithfully at Spirit of Deliverance C.O.G.I.C. where her father is pastor. Ronkeyuna is the visionary of *The Way God See Me*, a movement designed to encourage young women who have experienced low self-esteem, loneliness, feelings of rejection, and feeling unloved to empower them to success. She is a graduating senior at Grambling State University with a Bachelor's degree in Social Work.

To learn more about Ronkeyuna visit, www.wakeprayslaybook.com/ronkeyunagreen.

SHEARESE STAPLETON
Victoriously Unstoppable

I would say despite my premature entrance into the world, I turned out well. I was born two pounds three ounces at birth. Yes, I was a preemie. I was so tiny, I fit in the palm of my daddy's hand. But that did not stop me. I thrived through childhood and adolescence into a beautiful young woman, wife, and mother. Out of all those titles, mother was the hardest one to be.

I had a million preconceived notions on how to be a good mother, a saved mother, a strong mother, and most of all, the mother to the children I thought I could not have. Yet, I couldn't shake the negative voice that toyed with me day in and day out. It taunted me constantly, from telling me I was not worth the air I was breathing to telling me what I didn't deserve. I didn't deserve the promotion. I didn't deserve the house or the car. I didn't deserve the business. I didn't even deserve my life. The problem wasn't so much the voice inside my head, it was that I listened to it and allowed it to talk me into ruining my whole life.

It all came to a head when I decided I was invincible, I did not need anyone, and that I could do my life much better without anyone, especially my husband. My first act of ignorance was to file for divorce. My husband had not done anything to deserve my abandonment. I just thought I would be better off happily ever after alone. But God has a way of showing you who is in charge. He allowed arrogance and selfishness to take me to places I would never have visited if I'd only listened to the right voice.

The problem was that I didn't know who I was. I was sitting in church being told I was the head and not the tail but deep down inside, I didn't believe it. I couldn't feel it or embrace the truths that were being spoken to me because of the lies satan continued to speak to me. Like Eve in the Garden, he would constantly contradict every truth I embraced as false. I had already been deceived so I tried to hide myself because I was naked and exposed. Instead of running to the ark of safety, I ran in the opposite direction.

Desperate to see change in my life, I decided to go back

to school, pick up where I left off, and pursue a degree in social work. I had almost completed my early childhood degree when I had to go back to work. I was not the most successful juggler and working to pay rent, keep the lights on and school caused all of the balls to fall out of sync and crash to the floor. I would go home, lay on the couch, and watch television. There I would stay until the next morning. My car stopped working, so getting back and forth to work and class became an even bigger obstacle. I was overwhelmed, so overwhelmed that I found myself checking out; out of talking to people, out of being tangible to people, out of life. I stopped answering my phone and I wouldn't go to the door if anyone came knocking. I built up an emotional wall and refused to allow anyone in.

Of course, this alarmed my family members who suggested I get professional help. But what did they know? I didn't feel I needed to see anyone because I didn't feel like there was anything wrong with me. But, oh, how wrong I was! I needed to get to the root of my self-destructive behavior. I needed to talk to someone who was qualified to help me put the pieces of my life back together because I was telling all my business to anyone who would sit still long enough to hear. The fact of the matter was that I had so many unresolved issues: I was a problem child, I never felt like I belonged in my family because I was the oldest child whose father was different than the other two, if I told anyone they would think I was crazy...and the list goes on.

After my divorce life got real hard real fast. My decision to walk away from my husband created a ripple effect of negative consequences. My business declined. I lost my house and I almost lost my mind. But like most people, I kept trying to move forward every day as if there was nothing wrong. *"There is a way that seemeth right unto a man, but the end thereof are the ways of death"* Proverbs 16:25.

Despite my best efforts, I was left to move in with my sister who didn't have enough room for me and my children so they had to live with my ex-husband. I couldn't take care of myself so taking care of them was not an option. I was at the mercy of people telling me, a grown woman, what I could and could not do. It was too much for me to bear. I was unable to cope with my life and the twists and turns it was taking and I just completely lost myself. I couldn't understand why any of this was happening to me. It seemed everyone else was going on with their life and there I was, in my sad, broken down, wretched state. My self-esteem was at an all-time low. I was used to being able to at least take care of myself; buy my clothes, get my hair done, etc. But I didn't have, as the old saying goes, "two nickels to rub together".

I ended up in a women's shelter which was a harsh reality for me. Strangely enough, it was what I needed to help me get back on my feet again. You can imagine how difficult it was for someone who was a business owner for almost fifteen years to have had be subservient to people who didn't know my struggle. On the other hand, I formed bonds with other women there who, I could see, had been through much worse than I. I was in that shelter for almost six months but still, somehow, didn't learn all the lessons I needed to put my life back together. Just when I didn't think it could get any worse, I ended up going to stay with, yet, another family member.

This was truly rock bottom for me. I was experiencing what it felt like to be kicked, real hard, while I was down. I was emotionally abused by my family member and made to feel like a slave cooking and cleaning for them. But at my rock bottom, I finally had a "come to Jesus" moment. *"My sheep hear my voice, and I know them, and they follow me:"* John 10:27. Like the prodigal son who came to himself, I was able to wade through the fog of disobedience and find my way back to the light.

I sought the Lord and stopped trying to do things my way. I got therapy and began to compartmentalize my pain and stop allowing it to be an excuse for my behavior. God settled me and I didn't have to run from life any longer. Once I got still and settled, the blessings started coming. Someone at my church gave me a car. Yes, I said *gave* me a car. Three months later, I secured somewhere to live. I had a job and my life was finally flourishing again.

No one can tell me that God is not real. He literally saved my life. I no longer take medication for depression. With the help of my doctor, I was taught alternative ways to deal with stress and anxiety. I put the work in to discover who Shearese really was and I began to combat that voice that got me off track in the first place. Philippians 4:13 reminded me that *"I can do all things through Christ which strengtheneth me"*. I learned how to fight back with the word of God. Everyone was fighting for me, my pastor, my children, my family, but the time came when I had to fight for myself. I focused my attentions on what things were most important; my life, my children, and my relationship with God. I learned how to hear His voice again and that has made all the difference.

Listening to the wrong voice almost made me forfeit the gifts God placed on my life; the gift of song He put in me and he almost made me forfeit my promise. He promised to never leave me nor forsake me and He proved himself true. He was with me in my struggle. He was with me in the fire and what He birthed out of me because I made it through, the half has not yet been told.

With my new-found identity, I started a non-profit organization for mothers and women in crisis called *Mothers of Joy University* that empowers mothers to embrace their journey. My desire is that if I can prevent someone from going through the same struggles I went through, then my experience will not have been in vain. My life, would have, in some small way, been validated and given meaning. I instill in women that there is always someone on the other side of the struggle waiting for them to win and I can be that example of strength for them I didn't have when I needed it the most. The moral of this story is when the wrong voice comes to tell you that you are not worthy, I dare you to tell it, *"Yes I Am"* because you are Victoriously Unstoppable!

About Shearese

Shearese Nekail Stapleton is the CEO and founder of *Mothers of Joy University*, an organization the empowers mothers of all different backgrounds to embrace the journey of motherhood. Mothers of Joy University was birth when Ms. Stapleton realized that her mistakes and challenges could help others to avoid the pitfalls that could lead to divorce, homelessness, and depression.

Shearese has worked in Early Childhood development for over twenty-three years. She operated a group childcare and early "fives" preschool program to address the social, emotional, and spiritual develop of young children. She facilitated workshops, group coaching, and other trainings to cultivate heathy parent-child relationships through her Hearts at Home, Homemakers by Choice, Ministry of Motherhood, and Love & Logic programs. Shearese is currently the childcare instructor and coordinator for the House of Ester (Flint, MI).

To learn more about Shearese visit, www.wakeprayslaybook.com/shearesestapleton.

TRACEY WOLFE
Transformationally Unstoppable

There I was back in Winston-Salem, North Carolina going through another divorce from a man I thought was my soulmate, my friend, my husband forever. I was so devastated at my loss that I was totally unresponsive and the people around me only made me feel worse. I was miserable and I felt like I couldn't talk to anyone about my situation.

"You are too fat! You are too dark! You're too skinny! You are not good enough! You are dumb! You are stupid! You don't have anything to offer!" All these voices raced through my head daily. I felt like all hope was lost. I would be single for the rest of my life. I was a mother of two, twice divorced. No one in their right state of mind would love me. At that point I didn't

even love myself, so much so, I began doing things out of my character.

I started smoking cigars! You know the ones located by the register at the gas station counter? I would take a few puffs while strolling in the park or at the end of the day behind my house where no one could see me. I moved up to a whole cigar a day. First of all, I have never been a smoker, so for me to start a habit of smoking cigars was very drastic for me.

I pushed men away because I was afraid I would end up in another failed relationship. I described myself to men, those who attempted to approach me, as a beautiful Tiffany Box. *"I am wrapped in a pretty tiffany blue box with a beautiful bow on top, but the expensive gift that is supposed to be on the inside is broken and shattered into pieces. I'm broken. I'm worthless. You don't want me!"*

I would have thoughts of killing myself and I would hear a voice inside my head telling me *"you are such a failure you would fail at committing suicide."* I remember waking up feeling like I had never been asleep. I would be exhausted. My body felt like I had been fighting all night long.

Feeling embarrassed, I build up walls of isolation and refused to verbalize the pain. I tried to cover up my mental state until my doctor intervened. I was told I needed to see a psychiatrist because I was dealing with depression. Words cannot express the level of anxiety that I experienced. Depression? I thought I had hit an all-time rock bottom. Two marriages, two divorces, homeless, carless, and jobless *and* they wanted to put me on medication for depression. I was a walking mummy. I was going through life everyday existing but I wasn't living.

Reluctantly, I went to see the psychiatrist. He asked me a plethora of questions. Two questions stood out to me that I will never forget: (1) *"Are you a part of a church or social group?"* Feeling sorrowful, my response to him was *"Well, NO! We had our own church and since I moved back here I have stopped attending church. I'm tired of people asking me about him!"* Next question (2) *"What accomplishments are you proud of?"* With my head hanging down looking at the floor, I responded by telling him, *"Nothing!"* He rephrased the question and he asked, *"What are you most proud of?"* I looked up, stared at him, and responded with tears in my eyes and a smile on my face *"my girls!"*

From that session, I knew I needed to change. You know the phrase, "it's easier said than done?" Knowing I had to change and actually turning my life around for the better proved to be very difficult for me. There were days I didn't know if I brushed my teeth, combed my hair, or bathed my body. There were times I didn't know my own name. I heard people talk about God being a mind regulator. Now I had my own personal testimony.

I became aware of what I was dealing with, the battle of *my* mind. The battle of the mind wasn't new to me, but this attack was unlike any other I had ever experienced. I knew a transformation had to take place. I had to stop listening to the negative voices and thoughts in my head.

"And be not conformed to this world: but be ye transformed by the renewing of your mind, that ye may prove what is that good, and acceptable, and perfect, will of God" Romans 12:2.

The first thing I did was get back into church and begin applying the Word of God to my life. Meditating day and night, I began to feel vibrant and dream all over again. God brought back to my remembrance businesses that I had started, visions and goals He had placed in my heart.

"Delight thyself also in the Lord: and he shall give thee the desires of thine heart." Psalms 37:4

Doors began opening for speaking engagements, my personal styling services and other business opportunities. The more I began to speak, the fewer burdens I felt. The more I helped others, the more freedom I had over my life.

I remember the very last time I introduced my second ex-husband, before he got up to preached. I told the congregation, *"I don't want to be a public success and a private failure?"* That statement came back to my spirit from time to time just to remind me, *"A double minded man is unstable in all his ways"* James 1:8. I couldn't teach people to have a positive mindset, motiving them to go after their dreams, and I didn't apply those same encouraging words to my life. I couldn't teach people how to be transformational when transformation hadn't taken place in my own life.

The session with the psychiatrist brought clarity to my "why" …. my daughters! When I didn't have enough reasons to carry on for myself, I found some in them. They gave me the fuel I needed to get up in the morning and strive to be the best every day. I created personal affirmations for my children and I because I understood that death and life was in the power of our mouth. No longer did I walk around with low self-esteem ashamed of my past. I had a peace of mind realizing the past was a part of the process. My life experiences caused me to develop the mindset that I *CAN* do all things through Christ.

"Thou wilt keep him in perfect peace, whose mind is stayed on thee: because he trusteth in thee" Isaiah 26:3.

Evolving into the woman God has called me to be, I now have a greater appreciation for the Word of God. I had to let go of the anger, so I could love myself. Because God is love, I learned how to genuinely love everyone, yes, even my ex-husbands.

There are no regrets only lessons learned that formulate my success story. I can contribute who I am today to my laughter and tears, my good decision making and poor choices, my trials and my tribulations. I give credit to the bitter and the sweet, to being in love, the heartaches and the pain. I celebrate raising children with and without a father in the household. With no money in the bank and no business loans, my Lord and Savior Jesus Christ gave me witty inventions and new ideas to start my businesses. The collaboration of all these things has brought me to a victorious way of living.

I have no more bad habits. No more beating myself up with negative thoughts. I have taken dominion over my life and I have become a new creature!

"Therefore if any man be in Christ, he is a new creature: old things are passed away; behold, all things are become new" 2 Corinthians 5:17.

I am fearfully and wonderfully made and the joy of the Lord is my strength. I am no longer broken. I have transformed into a valuable woman. I am the head and not the tail. I am the lender not the borrower. I am living my life on purpose. I am here to inspire women to keep shining regardless of their circumstances. My mission is to encourage people, "It's okay to fail, but it's not an option to remain a failure." We all fall down; successful people get back up and try again.

"For a just man falleth seven times, and riseth up again." Proverbs 24:16.

Surround yourself with positive people that will push you back into the race. Seek wise counsel that will provoke you to aim for higher heights. Write the vison, make a plan, and execute until your dreams become a reality. On those days when you get distracted, focus on your "why" and remember God's promises for your life.

"And he shall be like a tree planted by the rivers of water, that bringeth forth his fruit in his season; his leaf also shall not wither; and whatsoever he doeth shall prosper" Psalms 1:3.

Your life will have challenges. Obstacles will come your way. You will have hurdles to jump, walls to climb, and rivers to cross, but your mindset should remain the same.... through all of this, I am still simply Unstoppable!

"Therefore, my beloved brethren, be ye stedfast, unmoveable, always abounding in the work of the Lord, forasmuch as ye know that your labour is not in vain in the Lord" 1 Corinthians 15:58.

About Tracey

Tracey Wolfe is a native of Winston-Salem North Carolina. She is the owner of Flawless Image-Beauty-Fashion where her passion is coaching people on their inner and outer beauty, and helping individuals with their personal brand and professional image development. As Chief Executive Officer of TRW Management, Tracey and her professional staff manage people, events & small businesses with excellence. She serves as a member of the Piedmont Triad Women's Forum, corporate partner with Dress to Success and is on the Board of Directors for Phenomenal Woman, an organization which ministers to battered women. Tracey is the author of "8 Ways to Raising Them to be Better Not Bitter" and is a part of numerous mentoring programs & outreach ministries. She is also the proud mother of two beautiful daughters. Tracey's mission is to empower men, women, boys and girls to Keep Shining 365 regardless of their circumstances!

To learn more about Tracey visit, www.keepshining365.com.

CONNECT WITH US

If you found this book helpful in any way, we would love it if you would leave a review or feel free to contact any of the authors via the information provided at the end of their stories.

Thank you for your support and remember...
YOU ARE UNSTOPPABLE!

CPSIA information can be obtained
at www.ICGtesting.com
Printed in the USA
FFOW01n1649100417
34341FF